Map for the heart

Map for the heart

Ida Valley essays

JILLIAN SULLIVAN

OTAGO UNIVERSITY PRESS
Te Whare Tā o Te Wānanga o Ōtākou

Published by Otago University Press
Te Whare Tā o Te Wānanga o Ōtākou
533 Castle Street
Dunedin, New Zealand
university.press@otago.ac.nz
www.otago.ac.nz/press

First published 2020
Copyright © Jillian Sullivan
The moral rights of the author have been asserted.

ISBN 978-1-98-859256-5

Published with the assistance of Creative New Zealand

Editor: Imogen Coxhead
Cover: Rachel Hirabayashi, *Central landforms*, acrylic on canvas. www.rachelhirabayashi.co.nz
Author photo: Darren Simmonds

Printed in New Zealand by YourBooks

for Brian

The loveliest places of all
are those that look as if
there's nothing there
to those still learning to look.

                    –*Brian Turner*

CONTENTS

Becoming Something Other

LATE AUTUMN, and once again it's time for the firewood we gathered through summer – jaunts across the paddock to the old willows, cracked and split in storms, for the branches they delivered on top of fence lines and into the damp gullies. Fire crackles and brightens the room at night, though in Auckland, perhaps, warm still rules. Here, the wind presses up to the windows, whoos and blusters around the house. The clouds foretell a time soon to come when snow will lie on the hills and rocks and, if the wind is from the north, on my boots on the verandah and the twigs for the fire.

Before my first big snowfall here, the locals had checked with me: 'Are you ready for the storm?' 'Yes,' I'd said, but I had shifted down from Motueka and didn't know the power of cold. On the first morning, the snowplough half-buried my car. Snow lay half a metre thick over my unprotected firewood pile. In the village, gutters collapsed under the weight of it, and in the hills, farmers and volunteers, helicoptered to the tops, tramped pathways in a chain to bring the sheep down to safety.

To live here is to come to terms with the dominance of nature. When the snow melted, the Ida Burn stream on my boundary thrashed and swirled over its banks. My paddocks, from the first ditch to the neighbour's hill, became one writhing stretch of water. When it was over there were new grey shapes by the trees, sifted sand delivered by the flood. I took Roman architect Vitruvius's words to heart. 'Where there is no pit sand, we must use the kinds washed up by rivers or by the sea,' he wrote over 2000 years ago, 'and other problems we must solve in similar ways.' Buckets of sand, carried from the stream, became part of the last coat of earth plaster on the house (one part sand, one part clay, one part straw, one part water, half a part sawdust). Rubbed on by hand, baked by sun, it became a thick, undulating shell protecting the straw walls from rain.

I didn't know what vernacular architecture was when I drew sketches for my strawbale home. I've since come to understand it's the architecture that arises from place. It fits the weather, the landscape, the culture, the materials, and is often built with community help.

The early Māori who first came to this tussock-covered valley built round huts thatched with tussock. The goldminers and farmers built with rock and earth and limestone. If there was timber to be had for floors and ceilings, it came on the ships that brought the pioneers here. My strawbale house echoes the high-pitched roofs of the early cottages. The straw came from a farm near Gore, the clay from a site thirty minutes up the valley, the lime from a quarry over the Pigroot, an hour away. The milk for the lime wash came in buckets from a farm across Rough Ridge in Gimmerburn, fetched one foggy morning when the mist made dark shapes of the cows and the gravel road curved into cloud.

In fact, strawbale building came out of a vernacular tradition. When the baling machine was invented in 1820, the people of Nebraska, a place where little timber was to be had, turned to what was available locally – bales of straw – and began to build with those, incorporating the new structure of bales into the age-old method of using straw and mud to build shelter.

Building one's own home is not just an enterprise of the past. British architectural historian Paul Oliver wrote in 2003 that vernacular dwellings, built by owners and inhabitants using locally available resources, are presently believed to constitute about 90 percent of the world's total housing stock. It is essential, Oliver said, that vernacular traditions are supported, to address our community and global shortage of housing. Bring on the earth, the straw and the grandmothers, I say.

The people who helped build my house came from across New Zealand, and also from right here: from next door, from up the road, from the next valley. When they walk in, the hints of their handprints are still in the walls. They know this house, from the scent of golden stalks to the acid cream of lime. Their kindness and strength is in this house, their mortality and mine in the walls that will continue beyond us, like the rock walls half formed into the sides of hills, the uncapped mud huts, the chimneys beside the Manuherekia – all testament to people who arrived and shaped a dwelling for themselves and their neighbours.

In the days after my marriage ended and before my shift to Central Otago and all that ensued, I thought of American mythologist Joseph Campbell's quote, that life is 'an unremitting series of deaths and births'. Old life gone. New life begins. Campbell spoke of the journey a hero must make – the quest that is chosen, or the path the reluctant hero must find. But how? And where?

Choosing

(for Nick and Bex)

How do you know
which hills and sky and water
will be your home,
the place where you long to return?

There's the unexpected beauty of light
in city structures on a lengthening night
beside the sea,
the dark of furrowed loam,
an alabaster cottage, sheen of calm tide
through a wheelhouse window.

What of a river? Under the resilient arms
of willows, whatever the water says
over brown and shining stones,
you'll know if it is meant for you.

How do you choose
which rocks and trees and soil
will be your own?

Sometimes just by standing still
there with your feet on earth where you have landed
you'll feel the way two cogs within you
settle into unison,
power your heart, gain traction.

And when a bird lifts in the sky above you
something in your own heart
flings forward with a gust of joy,
the way a hawk soars, wing-feathers fanned,
riding the currents of desire
in a wide blue territory of sky.

I first saw the Ida Burn from a bridge: a coppery, shining pathway bounded by trees. There'd been nothing to tell me the swampy piece of land for sale beside the main road had anything of such beauty. Only a scrawl of willows along the far boundary. The Ida Burn – it flows down the Ida Valley and, uniquely, is met by a stream flowing from the opposite direction, the Poolburn. Joined, it heads through the Poolburn Gorge between the Raggedy Range and Blackstone Hill, where viaducts rise and rail tunnels lead cyclists into the dark of the land and out again.

I'd looked for a piece of land with running water, because for seventeen years in Motueka I'd lived beside the sea. The light on water and the call of seabirds had been a constant solace to me. And when your life takes a sudden turn, it's the thread of things that can lead you through.

Starting over – we think we did that when we first left home, aged eighteen with a future yet to be shaped. If we were lucky, we already had some sense of a thread, like Ariadne's string, that we followed. A catch in the throat – ah, this is where I want to be, who I am, who I love.

Aged fifty-five, deposited once again on the shores of the childless, partnerless, soon-to-be homeless. This time round I was facing it all with hair going grey, body stiffer and a numb sense of hopelessness.

'Never let yourself be bitter,' friend and writer Joy Cowley reminded me. I took that piece of advice as if it were timber redefining my boundaries.

Loss. It comes to us in many ways. Comes silently, suddenly, or sometimes as if it is the last piece of a jigsaw put into place. There, and now it's time to go. Change is something else, though it has the same outcome. One is chosen, the other not. Yet there we are, walking into the unknown. And something in us arises to face it.

But why did you come *here*, people asked me – a young farmer at the pub, or a farmer's wife – a farmer herself, seeing to the lambing beat and three children while her husband was overseas.

'Because of the hills,' I'd say.

When all else fails, the light on the hills is unfailing; the ridges outlined in gold at sunset, and in the morning the folds and gullies blue, almost transparent, as the sun rises.

Land is cheap here because, as one traveller sitting in the local café with a very good coffee put it, 'I'm in the middle of nowhere.'

Yet nowhere is always somewhere – to the hawks cruising the

thermals above the Ida Burn, to the stolid Hereford crosses munching the ryegrass and timothy, oblivious to the rain. To the farmers bringing in an unexpected third crop of lucerne after a wet spring. And to the new people who find this valley, who find any valley in the middle of nowhere, which offers respite from a broken life or from that dull and awkward feeling that perhaps there is more to life – and perhaps it is here, with the sparrows thriving in the willows, the blue heron an arrow gliding towards the pond and the light changing on the rocky tors. Everywhere is a reminder that we are only a part of this world, not its dominator, and privileged to be here.

'And to be near my grandchildren,' I say.

Oh, family then. 'Where are they?'

'Queenstown.'

And then the snort, as if Queenstown – with its ragged mystical mountains, thronging streets, traffic maelstroms and art galleries open till almost midnight – is close by, is not another country to this village of approximately twenty-nine people.

Most likely many don't know of Ōtūrehua here on the high alpine plain on the old goldmining route to Dunedin.

A Christchurch writer, coming to stay for the first time, felt lost on the long stretch of the Ida Valley road heading towards the Hawkdun mountains. She stopped at Poolburn Pub, twenty-five kilometres down the valley from the village, and asked where Ōtūrehua was. The people in the bar shrugged. 'Where the poet Brian Turner lives,' she said. But they hadn't heard of him either. It was a shearing gang, we worked out later, unfamiliar with the people or places here, but at the time it only reinforced her sense of isolation.

'Ōtūrehua?' she said again. But perhaps if she'd said 'Oture', like the locals do.

Once there were mainly farmers here, and truck drivers. People who were born here or nearby. And now on a Friday night at the pub, having a pint alongside those who work on the land are imports from Auckland, Christchurch, Wellington, Tauranga, Dunedin, Motueka. The publican brings us out trays of free garlic prawns or chips or pizza. Rail-trailers might join us too. 'Where have you come from?' we ask – meaning Ōmakau or Wedderburn by bike, and also, which land do you call home? And if it's fine in the west, from the bar we can watch the Hawkduns glow tangerine with the setting sun.

Hammering in nails. I didn't know I would like it so much. Hour after hour, only thinking of that one silvered point and the rise and fall of my arm.

'The proper business of living is to enjoy life. To enjoy, to charge with joy.' I read that last week in my grandfather's book *I Say Sunrise* by Talbut Mundy. He wrote that in 1947, referencing Samuel Butler: 'All of the animals, excepting man, know that the principal business of life is to enjoy it.'

Hammering in nails, charged with joy. I felt it too when son-in-law Sam and I drove up to the building site and I climbed out in my work boots and jeans and buckled on my toolbelt. We lifted out the heavy drop saw and Sam turned the music on, the sun already up over Mt Ida and a whole day of building ahead of us.

Seven grandmothers helped in the building of my house. And four poets. Four artists. A magician, a Harley biker, a finance manager. Apart from Sam, only one other person – Pat Shuker, one of the grandmothers – knew how to build with straw, and she was seventy-three. You only need one builder.

'Why would you go and help someone you don't know?' one of Pat's friends had asked her.

'I can't have my own dream of a strawbale house yet, so I want to help someone else get theirs,' she'd told them. 'That's what you do, my generation anyway. If someone needs a hand, you get in and help them.'

Early in the building process when the walls weren't in, blue plastic tarpaulins flapped and surged in the wind and the straw was stacked seven high in the rooms. I didn't know how to keep going. Winter was only weeks away. The sky dwarfed the house, and the task of the house dwarfed me. Yet when they were needed, people came. According to American essayist and novelist Marilynne Robinson, 'The great truth that is too often forgotten is that it is in the nature of people to do good to one another.'

When it came to lime plastering – covering over the timber frame, the walls of straw, the earth plaster – this time it was a reckoning between the house and myself. How much had I learnt from Sam about paying attention, about getting it right? How much had I learnt from those who came to help, about generosity of time and energy, about not giving up? I climbed the scaffold alone, hauled up buckets of lime plaster by rope and picked up my hawk and trowel, the concrete mixer rumbling beneath me. I began to lay on the creamy golden finish. I had faith in the arc of my trowel, the new strength in my arms. The rare joy of plastering, of spreading this simple cloak on mud, the house transformed again.

To live here is not so different from anywhere else. Finding a home is more about finding a place where you can be who you believe you are. If you take care of that inner need, then the home around you is simply the place that gives you rest, and the people nearby will be the ones who appreciate you. Intrinsic to this is that our communities are places where we can be recognised, acknowledged.

But how to live? It is a problem. And the solutions we come up with – if they line up with our values, then there's where we'll find 'home'.

I believed I was capable, that we all are capable in some way, of helping build a natural house. I believe our homes are best made from simple, natural, sustainable materials. Out of these beliefs, a strawbale home. A community in which I belong. And many possibilities to charge with joy.

The cold here unites people. We understand the need for wood. The need for rain unites us. And snow lays its mantle over all. I rise from my desk and go out when flakes begin to fall. Their rapturous descent is still a wonder to me, that vibrance of white on green and the world of grass and willow forever becoming something other.

With lime wash

Rough walls become smooth, luminous.
It's not so much covering
over, hiding flaws, but a building up of
radiance and sure, the walls still
curve and dip under your hand,
there's mud and straw,
you know how things arise –
yet to walk in and feel
that presence of light
is to know how things
transform.

Want is a thing that unfurls unbidden,
Kingsolver says, but *needs* –
I can think of no other fineness
than to build with earth, brush

light from rock, and there rest
dreaming after a day by clinking
stones, while overhead a pipit
sings.

Between Lands

THERE'S A MOMENT on the ferry crossing, mid-journey, when a bird hovering over the charcoal water turns and flies towards us, wings outspread. This bird, mollymawk, suspended between waves and an apricot sky. The bird turns again, and the boat speeds on towards a bank of clouds, the plume of them covering the island, Rakiura, where tomorrow I'll be teaching.

When the ferry motored past the last ramparts of the South Island, the last rocks, I lifted my phone to take a photo and saw the place I'd stood seven years before, newly on my own. I'd driven to Bluff because it was the southernmost end of the South Island, the furthest I could drive. I thought that would be a place to start, to get my bearings. And I'd stood on that ground and looked out at the ocean and wondered what would become of me. Where would I make a home? On the ferry, I salute that memory of my unknowing self. And now we're travelling beyond what I had imagined my life to be, heading full tilt into the waves towards a land of small coves, dark bush, birds and the ever-lapping sea, where people when they first meet you ask, 'How was your crossing?'

My granddaughter Estella, who is just three, lives on another island, Waiheke. She lives ten hours away from me – a two-hour car trip, a two-hour wait for the plane, a two-hour flight, an hour at the airport, an hour on the bus, an hour finding my way to the ferry, an hour crossing the sea, and then the bay and the dock, the green furled hills and a small girl with curls and a hesitant smile holding her father's hand.

I want to dismiss some facts about being older. You do not stop yearning. You do not stop wanting to find someone beside you when you turn. You do not stop remembering the clothesline with the tiny singlets and handmade pinafores and hand-washed stripy jerseys. The small people who wore them no longer exist in any cell form on this earth, but are now six foot and bearded, or have long shiny hair and a child on their lap, or are walking their dog on a beach you don't know, where stars are out and flax rattles in a squiffy breeze. There are new smaller ones tucked up asleep, the books read, the apples eaten, the teeth cleaned, the water drunk, the nappies on. At home alone I bring in an armload of wood, for stars mean frost. The curtains closed, the lamps on and the quiet of a thick-walled house saying *shhhh, all is well*, and it is.

The small girl, Estee, lives with her parents who are also isolated on their island – from sisters and brothers, and parents and grandparents, and aunts and uncles, and from friends they once knew who knew them. And they too are saying the goodnight story and passing the lidded cup of water and whispering, if not aloud, *all is well*. Outside the punga ferns brush against the verandah post, the white shells glimmer on the steps, and further down the road past the fish and chip shop and the pizza cart and the swings and climbing tower, the quiet waves lift and curl like breath onto the sand, the shells with their rounded white backs to the sky -- and far away my own mountains with their white sides glisten under the moon.

On the first morning, before teaching, I walk down to the sea with my coffee. The sand is damp and flat and the sea calm. Grey like the sky. These are the quiet few moments before the hard work and the journey of the day begins. Somehow, as I walk along the beach, there needs to be a transformation, from interior dweller to leader. From going mad sinking into my own psyche to helping others sink into theirs. Gulls careen across the bay. I cross the playground and walk up the street to the library door.

In the Gulf of Mexico there is an island called Isle de Jean Charles, and it is slowly disappearing into the sea. It is tethered to the mainland by a five-kilometre road, and there the sea eats and eats until only a ragged gravel edge remains. A child can stand there, bare feet in the water. But the school bus will no longer travel that watery highway, and on the island the hurricane-ruined houses stand empty and soggy mattresses lie on abandoned lawns. There are grandchildren and grandparents there too, almost everyone related, but where will they go? They too are standing at the bottom of the world, wondering what will become of their lives.

On Waiheke Island I wasn't sure of my direction as I drove. Estee, clipped in her carseat, watched out the window.

'There's the supermarket we went to yesterday,' I said. 'There's the road to your kindy. And there's the road to the beach. Shall we go swimming later?'

'Grandma, I'm a bit shy of you.'

I look up at her brown eyes in the rear-vision mirror.

'We don't see each other enough. I live at the bottom of New Zealand and you live at the top. Do you know "Baa Baa Black Sheep"?'

'Baa baa black sheep, have you any wool?' We sing across the island.

One of my students, Chris, owns the restaurant on Rakiura with his wife. He said it only takes one good person in a small community and things get done. 'We built this hall', he said. 'We sawed the timbers and worked in the weekends. People did what they knew. Christchurch wants a conference centre. They're a city, and they ask – who's going to do this for us? Our hall here is the equivalent of a four-million-dollar centre. People in cities forget they can help one another, they can do things. They ask instead, who's going to do this for us?'

What I want to know is, how do you hold everything in your heart? The toetoe frosted silver and snow beginning to fall in dizzy spirals, and a granddaughter's arms linked around your neck, right there beside the sea, and knowing you are it, you are Grandma.

When the class stood outside to watch the sand and the wavelets furl and unfurl, the temperature dropped. The rain changed from a shower that was dampening to rain that was continual and wetting. Wet jeans on thighs, the rain windblown towards the harbour, and cold legs, cold wet hands, wet notebooks. The sea and sky at one with this. I remember how elemental life is on an island. If there is a storm, you cannot leave. The island has the final say.

When I go to leave my granddaughter's island, her parents are at work. I must drive her to day-care and help her take off her sandals at the door and carry her backpack in and place it on the table. I sit with her on the carpet in a circle while Ginny finishes reading a story about frogs. Estee's face is lifted to the story. I hope she forgets, momentarily, that when I say goodbye, I am leaving the island. I know, in a way that she doesn't, that when I return she will be someone else. There'll be another story, not the frogs, and her sandals outgrown and perhaps some other favourite lunch. When I climb onto the boat it feels as if it's forever. It is like forever to a three-year, two-week-and-one-day-old girl. And to me.

Rakiura has steep humped sides. Even if the water rises, the island's going nowhere fast. Waiheke is the same. That much we can be grateful for.

At the writing workshop, in our cramped room lined with books and the long table and chairs, we write and write.

'This morning one of the guests said my fire alarm woke her,' Raelene says. 'I thought, fire alarm? No, it was the kiwis.'

'Do they sound like this?' I ask. '*Kweet kweeet kweet*? I heard that outside my window.'

'No, it's more *kwiiiiiiiireet kwiiireeeet*.'

'No, like this,' another said, and ended in a rumble like a man clearing his throat.

Outside rain, sun, wind, mist, rain.

Everyone has loss. Some, great loss. This is the one truth of writing groups, for this is the well we draw on for courage and humour as well as for grief. To go back and back for the strength to hold now. To hold.

We write a poem, one line each, like donating a square for a quilt to keep someone else warm. 'The sea is … An island is … Choose one,' I say, and I write too. There is silence, then slips of paper passed along the table.

The sea is our borderline; it tells us where we are …

On the last morning I teach at the local school. Thirty-two students. Not one farm on this island; the living comes from the sea. 'My dad's a fisherman,' a young girl tells me. 'And mine,' says another. Some students come from Ireland, and Christchurch, and Queenstown. Some tell me, 'I'm eleven years old. I've lived here all my life.'

There's a boy who doesn't want to write. He *wants* to write. He is full of story, but how to start?

'Just start,' I tell him, like I tell my adult students. 'It doesn't matter how you start. Something will come. You don't know what that is. You can trust it will come, though.'

He grips his pen harder. It's poised over his book. Then half a minute before the timer goes off, he writes two sentences. He doesn't want to read them out loud. When the teacher says he must, he looks to me as if I will save him.

Life will only get harder, I want to tell him. One day you'll have to go off to boarding school, you'll have to stand up, put your creative endeavours in front of those who don't know you. Better to begin here, in this small circle of islanders. Better to feel what it's like to take that leap – the fear, and then the achievement – now.

He begins to read. A small step, and I am overwhelmed again at how much courage a child needs to live. His voice is clear and measured and strong. Hearing him, one would not know the clenched pen.

'This is how it is for writers,' I tell the class. 'Sometimes you don't know what to say, and you have to say it.'

Seven years ago, when I left the North Island for the South Island, my blue car was packed to the ceiling (minus the soup pot, which I'd given to my daughter). Blustery wind in Wellington. A photo shows me with my hair blown across my face. The air sharp, fresh, though it was December and summer. And all along there was a home waiting for me on the other side, though I didn't know it then. A home that needed to be imagined, constructed, committed to, but it arose. I didn't know I would become strong in my arms and legs. I could have sailed from north to south and emerged as practical and capable on the other side because it was necessary, and it happened anyway. As it was, I took my positive and naïve self and blundered into the building process and then grew stronger. And now I have a home, far from my children.

When I lived in Wellington there were three children out of my five living in the same city, and Estee not born. Now my children and grandchildren live in different localities the length of New Zealand, and in Australia. Is it possible we could all live near one another again? Some would have to change islands, or country, move from snow to tropical, or sea to mountains, from city to village, from mainland to island. I would have to leave my handmade house, because who would choose to live in the coldest valley in the country? Where there are limited jobs and you take turns cleaning the public toilet and it's a long way to buy groceries? If we could all have chosen the same place … but we have grown idiosyncratically and have flown like particles to metal attraction. I cannot change a thing.

Yet how do you hold it all in one heart, one island?

On Isle de Jean Charles, in the southern bayous, some of the islanders want to stay and some have already gone. What they hope for is to be together. The government has purchased a 222-hectare sugarcane farm an hour's drive away to relocate the community to.

'What are they going to do when they get there?' asks 81-year-old Theo Chaisson, interviewed for the *Independent*. These islanders have always made their living from the sea. 'You think they'll have oysters in their backyard, speckled trout, red fish, shrimp? No.' Yet they'll be joined again by pathways, from grandparent to grandchild, friend to friend.

The binds of a land lived in for seven generations hold strong. Though this land was once a forest of oak and fir, and now smells of the rot of salt-infused trees, there are those who don't want to go. 'I'll tell them, "No, no, no",' says Chaisson. Maybe only his grandchildren will grow up amid the scent of sugarcane.

We are a turbulent world, one criss-crossed by those who leave, those who search for a new home, hearts wracked by memories of those they leave behind, and their land, but also by the effort of living with such loss. Of being disunited.

I walk away from my granddaughter to the car, then to the ferry. I stand on the aft deck for the crossing, facing the sea, arms crossed over my stomach for balance. I watch the waves churn and the island recede, bearing witness to the distance lengthening between us. One small bay becomes an island, becomes a dark horizon, becomes one island among headlands and other islands, becomes diminutive in the expanse of sea and sky. Behind me the obelisks of the city rise.

How do we live without the people we love? It is a question that has no simple answer or solution. We are condemned to loneliness. We leave or are left by the small ones, or the old ones, or our own ones. The landscape changes inexorably: rivers we once swam in now cannot be entered, trees we once loved have been felled. There were open spaces we once gazed across, now blocked by fences, by malls. We live with this too.

I place my suitcase on the asphalt at the city end. People brush past me. I don't know how to carry on. How to walk my way to the bus. Back to my life of mountain, valley, tussock, hawk.

On Rakiura, before I left, the sea was grey, the surface roughened by wind. A low surge of water rolled over itself into foam. The boats faced the shore, their ropes leading to matching orange buoys, looped in that space between air and water. The boats lightly held on the surface of the sea.

Ancient Land

THERE ARE SOME WHO SAY of the parched golden ecosystems of our Central Otago drylands, 'Nothing there.' A desert (so profaning deserts); a land that may be of some use to humans, of some economic importance for the short time of a person's life, only if water is poured upon it. And to hell with the existence of what is there – the unknown, frequently unseen, unheralded plants from the age of dinosaurs: useful, in their brilliance of adaptation and beauty, in the full sense of community. At Butchers Dam I'm reminded of Brian Turner's poem 'Deserts, for instance': 'The loveliest places of all/ are those that look as if/ there's nothing there/ to those still learning to look.'

In considering the dread and power of a flooded river, American writer and environmentalist Wendell Berry wrote, 'One must simplify it in order to speak of it,' even 'to look at it'. This simplification of what is there, this ignorance of ignorance, is partly why five of us, aged fifty-eight to eighty and all committee members of the Central Otago Environmental Society (COES), gather at Flat Top Hill dryland reserve to pay homage to plants. To the smallest of plants, ones that take getting down on knees to peer at as if into far constellations through a telescope. There we are: president Brian Turner, treasurer Evelyn Skinner, committee members Michael Harlow, Matt Sole and myself (secretary). Matt, with a background in conservation and archaeology, is our tutor for the afternoon.

COES is known for its dedication to rivers – our river the Manuherekia in particular – and we have an Environment Court hearing in the near future over the neighbouring Lindis River. We're seeking a health-preserving minimum flow for the river. All people, wherever they live, ought to care for their own river and stand up for it and be a voice alongside it. But it's not only rivers that are threatened here in Central. Our land is the most threatened ecosystem in New Zealand, its dry hills seen as 'a wasteland', a resource in need of irrigation. But what is here? I can't name all the plants or say how they live. Plants like *Olearia odorata* with its musical name, its twig-like persistence in the heat, its silvery leaves and small, fragrant white flowers. I live here in these golden hills, in this 'world of difference', as the council touts, anguished by the loss of tussock lands (whose rippling shine I know) to the green rye of dairy fodder, but ignorant of what else lives and thrives in its own way here and is threatened, side-lined, simplified and considered of little importance.

Perhaps it was reading American lepidopterist and author Robert Michael Pyle's comment: 'If we have no clear idea of what went before, we are more likely to accept things as we find them, no matter how degraded they may be.' And that made me think of Brian's account of the Mackenzie country's lost Ōhau River in his autobiography *Somebodies and Nobodies*. I had no idea of the existence of that river, the 'clarity and fuming force' of it. I knew only the serene, bright blue canals from my road trips down south to visit grandchildren, and saw in the canals a sluggish, sky-reflecting beauty.

'The Ohau was a boisterous, belligerent river,' writes Turner,

> full of big boulders and white, sometimes green-streaked stones; in some sections the bottom was littered with polished lumps of earth's masonry. Alf said some of the pools looked as if the water ran over the ruins of Roman temples. The river's surface flexed, bumped, bulged. If ever a river could be said to hiss and roar, have muscles, it was the Ohau. It was a heavyweight boxer, both mesmeric and appalling. I was entranced by its power and also fearful.

I didn't know the wild river that had been sacrificed for the canals. I didn't know what had been lost to us forever. If a writer doesn't know his or her own world enough to bring it to readers, how then will people know what is there and what has gone? 'Recognizing loss,' as Pyle says, 'we may even act to prevent future loss.' Foremost as a writer, then, I had asked Matt to show us the dryland ecosystem he knows and loves.

We stand in the carpark next to Butchers Dam and look across to the shrub-textured land of Flat Top Hill, over to the hills of farmland on the slopes of the Old Man Range. Ploughed, over-sown, fertilised, irrigated – 'before they even knew what was there, what they'd taken away,' says Matt. 'How do we protect our world of difference? In twelve years, it's gone green before my eyes.' He stands there a moment looking across the valley. 'Flat Top Hill is a modified landscape, one of our few lowland areas in conservation. We've got the dregs but that's all we've got. There's no intention by council to identify any other areas of significance above existing conservation areas,' he says. 'And then, to make sure threatened native species didn't intrude on so-called development, there had to be a half-hectare block of contiguous listed threatened plant species. Native plants wouldn't exist in blocks like that in the wild,' he adds. 'Maybe you'd get it with California thistle, or gorse.'

He goes on to say the Central Otago landscape is the closest thing to a desert New Zealand has. 'The Old Man Range lifts the arctic winds and dumps them over the Hawkduns. Along with block mountains to the east and west it keeps this area sheltered in the rain shadows of the mountains.' So here we have Central – the driest area in New Zealand, lying just east of the mountains of Fiordland – the wettest area in New Zealand.

We begin our tour by walking along the edge of Butchers Dam. It's a hot, fine day but, typical of those who live in the Ida, Brian and I have come with jackets, woolly hats, even thermals. Matt is the most sensibly dressed, in T-shirt and shorts, but Brian and I never trust that summer means it will stay hot. For now, our jackets are tied around our waists. We stop and peer into the opaque depths of the water. The dam has an algal bloom; it's like looking at pea soup, swirling with a murky haze. And beneath the water, a history I hadn't known of either – the dammed Butchers Creek, and along with it part of a community, including Butchers Gully Hotel from the goldmining days. It's said that when the water is low you can still see the chimneystacks of the stone hotel glimmering beneath the surface.

The 813 hectares of Flat Top Hill Conservation Area was purchased by the Department of Conservation (DOC) in 1992. It was originally seabed, as was most of Central. Some 20–25 million years ago the sea reached inland as far as Ranfurly, Naseby and Tarras. When it receded this whole district, from St Bathans to Roxburgh, evolved into a wetland complex, Lake Manuherekia – a series of lakes and swamps with a subtropical climate complete with eucalyptus trees and crocodiles. A fragment of a crocodile's jawbone was found protruding from a low cliff near St Bathans in sediments estimated to be 16–19 million years old. And more recently, fossilised teeth and bones from a giant prehistoric bat were found in St Bathans and named *Vulcanops jennyworthyae*, for the St Bathans' Vulcan Hotel and the scientist who discovered the remains. Right here on the shores of Butchers Dam, Matt tells us, are ancient fossil soils, palaeosols, multi-coloured soils formed during that sub-tropical era. They were exposed by the goldminers' sluicing and are now protected in this reserve.

But it's the plants I want to know, and as soon as we are off the concrete structure of the dam Matt bends to show us the humblest of plants – the almost homeless tumbleweed lichen *Chondropsis semiviridis*. It looks like something crumbled on the ground, and when we bend to pick some up it has the fragile, bony structure of lichen, and yet it is completely self-sufficient. A life tumbled about on the earth and rocks by the wind. I'm pleased to find it again and again on our walk, something I now know exists and can name.

'Lichen is an ancient plant,' Matt says. 'Algae and fungi living in a symbiotic relationship.' And it's a good monitor of air clarity. 'Cities don't have lichen – the pollution stuffs them up. After rain the lichens are greener. Now they're parked up in hibernation.' *Chondropsis* is usually yellow-green. The shreds in our hands are a dusty yellow-brown. I wouldn't have known it for a living plant, and place the threads back on the soil.

'Most people first looking up at this hill will see thyme, briar, rocks,' Matt says. 'But this is a knee-high forest – a very misunderstood region. And if you look, you'll see the natives are regenerating. The native grass *Elymus solandri*, now it's no longer being grazed, is coming up through the thyme.' And I see it, the graceful, drooping, seed-laden heads of the grass that used to sway and bend in the breeze on the hills before the exotic grasses browntop and sweet vernal were introduced. Here on these protected hectares, species of *Elymus* are gaining space, threading their stems through the dry aromatic thyme and reaching above it.

The thyme is everywhere. The pungent spiky herb covers the land in browning scrawls, flushing purple in the spring. It's allelopathic, Matt tells us, producing a toxin that stops other plants growing unless it can be out-competed. Pines are the same, he says: 'The monoculture of a pine forest – it's like walking through a morgue, the past native vegetation out-competed for life-sustaining light.'

What sticks in my mind later is not the plants themselves but Matt's reverence and loyalty to them. His protective passion. Passion that leads to knowledge, and knowledge to action. How he led us across a slope, Michael taking care to balance on the rocks, Evelyn sure with her stick, Brian agile from his mountaineering days, and me in a tangle of jacket and knapsack clambering onto a high ledge beside Matt. He lifted a small chain of fern in his hand for us to see: *Asplenium flabellifolium*, the necklace fern. One of thirteen fern species inhabiting Flat Top in apparent contradiction of this semi-arid dryland system.

I sit here while I write this with my door open to the long poignant calls of the sheep separated from their lambs in the woolshed early this morning. The ewes up there now on Rough Ridge, bereft in the hard light on the slopes. I know that terrain: the small ponds cupped in folds on the ridge, the ewes and lambs in the shelter of monolithic tors, and the mothers alone now where the rocks hold the heat and the grass crackles underfoot after the drought.

I do not wish to know the fate of the male lambs in detail. The female lambs were driven back up the road this morning. They'll be knee deep in purple-flowered lucerne. The male lambs left on the red trucks I've seen going up and down the valley, the 'store lambs', gone to Canterbury for further fattening and then to the works, as they were always destined to, even as they each roamed with their mothers, sheltering by her woolly panting sides in drought and wind and hail alike, following her blindly along the age-worn trails on the side of the hill towards the drafting gate.

When I think of what we face – climate disruption, extreme weather events, the ongoing wrench of commercialisation into the heart of the wild, rivers dammed, insect-haven trees sprayed, tussock burnt – the thought of people like Matt Sole brings hope. Here there are a few, passionate in their own sphere, who do what they can. And sometimes that means against the status quo – doggedly inquiring of the district council or the regional council or the government, why is this happening? And suggesting what needs to be done instead.

Perhaps this land does look desert-like, but it wasn't always so. After the time of the swamps, with the climate changing and cooling, there were forests and, in the lowland areas, vast reaches of tussocks and native grasses. But by 1911, after a combination of frequent fires and constant over-grazing, a million hectares of Central Otago land had been left 'desert-like', according to a 1995 article in the *New Zealand Journal of Ecology*. The authors quote A.S. Mather: 'The desertification of Central Otago has been described as one of the most dramatic examples of land degradation to have resulted from European expansion overseas during the nineteenth century.'

Flat Top Hill had 150 years of pastoral grazing before DOC took it over. Modified by exotic grasses and chewed out by rabbits and sheep. The 'dregs' of lowland Central, as Matt put it. But now there's a rich plant remnant diversity. And though there are still introduced species here, there are 180 native species in this reserve, including the thirteen ferns. Of the introduced species, thyme and the thorny sweet briar dominate. I also recognise viper's bugloss, Californian thistle, St John's wort and the grey-leafed hieracium.

'From a soil ecology point, *Hieracium pilosella* or mouse-ear hawkweed is not too much of a problem, but for farmers it displaces grasses,' Matt tells us. 'Though the deciduous "king-devil" species leaves the soil it colonises bare over winter, subject to freeze–thaw cycles that cause erosion.'

I had seen what looked like bare earth on the sheep stations I walked over, on Blackstone Hill and North Rough Ridge. In one area I'd come across a patch of grass so luxuriant I'd asked the farmer what was different. He replied, 'There's no hieracium there.' And I realised, looking down, that what I thought I'd been walking over – close-cropped, drought-affected grass – was indeed large tracts of hieracium, its small flat leaves colonising the earth and preventing other plants from thriving.

Hieracium pilosella, or, as it's now known, *Pilosella officinarum*, by the 1990s was the most widespread and significant introduced weed in our native grasslands. Seeds were probably introduced alongside exotic grass seeds when tussock lands were burnt and over-sown. The lovely, wind-curving tall tussocks of the *Chionochloa* species disappeared from the high-country pastoral areas, and in the bare sites left exposed, invasive, grazing-tolerant species like hieracium thrived. Like thyme, it's allelopathic. It smothers and displaces small native herbs and grasses, acidifies the soil nearby and makes life hard for the browntop and sweet vernal the farmers prefer.

I wondered later if this plant was in fact a herb with medicinal properties. Its name was a clue – hieracium from the Greek word *hierax* for hawk. One website explains that Pliny the Naturalist believed hawks ate the plant to strengthen their eyes. I find no hieracium salves for eyes, but plenty of online evidence of it being used as a diuretic, as a cure for respiratory illnesses from asthma to whooping cough, boiled in milk for haemorrhoids, bruised and bound to any cut or wound to staunch bleeding and bring antibiotic protection and, as Culpeper wrote in his seventeenth-century *Complete Herbal*, as a 'wound herb for wounds inward and outward'. For various requirements, steep five to ten grams of the dried plant in a litre of boiling water, strain, and drink two glasses a day ...

While we're on the subject of introduced invasive species, Matt shows us the yellow-flowering stonecrop or *Sedum acre*, a low-growing succulent mat of fleshy green stems and yellow flowers, introduced in New Zealand in 1904. 'It's a successful coloniser from sea level to 2000 metres,' Matt says. 'It pops out seeds, and if you break it it will propagate vegetatively. When the television tower was put on the Old Man Range, they took gravel from down here, and brought stonecrop with it.' Matt spent ten years, on and off, trying to eradicate it in the Kopuwai Ranges when working for DOC. 'You can kill it, but eradicate it? Never.'

When a plant catalogue lists something as deer resistant, rabbit resistant, drought resistant and easy to grow, but says it can smother slower-growing alpine plants and is so tough it can grow on the walls and roofs of houses, you know you're in trouble. Or, as Matt has found out, if it's in the wrong place, you can't kill it. Over the centuries, stonecrop has gathered uses and names: Golden Moss, Biting Stonecrop, Prick Madam, Wallpepper. The name Welcome-Home-Husband-Though-Never-So-Drunk supposedly meant the plant, dried and powdered, enhanced virility. Other herbalists recommend the leaves split in two and the inner surface placed on corns or warts to remove them, though Culpeper warned, 'It ought not to be put into any ointment, nor any other medicine.'

At 6.30 in the morning the sheep are still baaing. An over-lapping deep vibration in the early dawn; a massed choir of loss. I think of the farmers to whom this country is as familiar as their dogs' faces, and this routine and swell of life cycles of parting and rebirth familiar too. A fertiliser truck rattles past on the road, for there are also crops to be taken care of – the choumolier for winter. While I turn in my bed on a morning of deep frost, the farmers will be out there, shifting an electric fence line or feeding out in slow, concentric circles on a glassy field. That wild innocence of the sheep and the rough-coated Hereford crosses, who cannot wonder at their place in all of this. The sheep who nip the sweet fresh lucerne under the pale morning sky, while beyond them the mountains light up with a pink glow, as if lit from within. The three orphan lambs the neighbours bottle-fed keep grazing, heads down, oblivious to the noise and the calling of the sheep across the road from them. It's perhaps beyond their ken, this fretting and baaing of the mothers, and the grass after last week's rain is juicy and cool on the lambs' tongues.

When you know something, you can't unknow it. Six months ago I watched a YouTube clip of sheep being pushed down a chute towards the freezing works killing room. I saw their panic, how they tried to turn back, flinging themselves over those pushed in behind them, and I realised: they want to live. I turned the video off. I said to myself, I can't take any part in this again. In doing so I joined my father, who lived as a vegetarian from the age of nine following a school trip to the Waingawa Freezing Works.

'Topography and aspect determine biodiversity,' Matt says. He indicates a rocky tor up the hill from our path. On its shady side, green thrives – there are tussocks, coprosmas, ferns, matagouri, *Olearia odorata*. He points out a gully to us: 'It's too steep to have been grazed and acts as a fire refuge, as rain is diverted into it. Its orientation means it's shady and not so affected by the sun, and that means more diversity.'

Closer to our path is a large rock, warmed by sun, and in front of it and clinging onto it a sprawling, flattened plant with interlacing grey-speckled branches, small green leaves and silvery spiky tips. *Melicytus alpinus*, Matt tells us. Porcupine shrub. He lifts a tangled branch to show us the purple-splashed white berries beneath it. I remember this plant now from up on top of the Hawkduns. The white blueberries.

'The skinks and geckos live in the crevices of the rock and feed off these berries,' Matt tells us, 'and in return the lizards scatter the seeds.'

'Oh, I know *this* one,' Evelyn says. She bends to a small plant with shiny light-green leaves and five-petalled pink flowers, a delicate trace of colour beside the path. A plant I might have walked right by. 'It's one of the finest bitters,' Evelyn says. 'I learnt about it on the herbal course I'm taking with Isla Burgess.' The plant is *Centaurium erythraea*, a 'pure bitter' as Isla says in her book *The Biophilic Garden*: 'This plant is small, simple, delicate, yet when you taste any part of it – it is intense. A bitter bombshell explodes in your mouth.'

We pass by matagouri, *Discaria toumatou*, that thorny companion to high-country tramping. It's our only thorned native, a threatened plant in the North Island but prevalent in the South Island, though under threat. It's not pretty. It doesn't have graceful arching green leaves. It will never be an emblem on our national flag or sports outfits. But in its own secretive ways it adds to the richness of diversity in this hard-won life in the drylands. Its long thorns and impenetrable branches form a protective shield for lizards and birds that rest and nest within its armour. When it sheds its leaves in a drought the stems and thorns carry out photosynthesis, and below the ground its roots, in a symbiotic relationship with fungi, fix nitrogen, allowing it to support itself without irrigation or fertilisers. What's more, it enriches the ground, to the benefit of other plants. Its sap is sweet, its flowers fragrant. And yet, Matt tells us, the District Plan allows landowners to spray hectares of matagouri, in the process destroying not only this thorny plant but also the grey-leafed divaricating shrubs that live alongside it, the *Melicytus* and *Coprosma propinqua*, all of them home to insects and birds. 'You're taking out a whole system,' says Matt.

Not everyone can see the matagouri's right to existence. 'This stuff makes gorse look like sheep's wool,' Cameron Slater wrote in his blog, Whale Oil. 'Its only purpose is to provide a huge volume of prickles. A farmer got rid of some on his farm and it cost him $10,000 and fake remorse …' Demonstrating once again what a hockey coach of Brian's said to him in the 60s: 'It's not the ignorance of some people that astounds. It's the f— extent of it.'

'Progress and decline,' Brian says to Matt. 'What do we have here, and what will we end up with?'

'Until we take in the wellbeing of all parts of the environment,' Matt replies, 'we're never going to take care of the world as it needs to be.'

Matt, Evelyn, Michael, Brian and I stand there beside the matagouri. There's thyme in the air and the hot breath of wind on the stones and rocky soils, where the tumbleweed lichen settles and stirs, settles and stirs at our feet. A shadow passes over us and we tip our faces up. A white-breasted, black-backed gull floating in a blue sky.

'To see *into* the natural world beneath our feet and the world around us,' Michael Harlow writes to me later. 'Such a fine reminder of our deep kinship with Nature; and a re-awakening to the fact that we too are part of the history of being. Looking at seed scatterings almost microscopic, leaf configurations, rock formations, and constellations of pebbles, and flowers and their colour-conversations; and patches of salt-sand risen over mega years to the surface … And most revealing I think from this walk into the landscape, how the history of our being is about *relationship* to everything there is in the world.'

On a stretch of white salty earth we kneel to examine a rare plant, New Zealand's smallest grass, the critically endangered *Puccinellia raroflorens*. Across the bleached earth the grass looks like smudges, its fine leaves half covered in soil. This is a plant with most things against it, except for its resoluteness in the face of saline soils, freezing temperatures and burning hot sun. The salt pans are formed, scientists think, from the weathering of the ancient schist rocks and a combination of heat and low rainfall. There were once 40,000 hectares of salt pans in the Maniototo basin. Now there are less than 100 hectares, scattered over thirty sites and increasingly under threat from salt-tolerant weeds and stray irrigation. In these few sites there are perhaps only 1000 plants of *Puccinellia* left in the world.

On the path home Matt stops to pull out a vagrant wilding pine. He points out a yellow-green shrub with bunched, papery-white flowers. It stands firm surrounded by tussock and thyme. After the tiny grass, it seems sturdy, unthreatened.

'*Ozothamnus*,' says Matt, '*leptophyllus*.'

'Behold, Ozymandias,' says Brian.

'Jesus, Shelley,' says Michael.

And yet, here we are. Travellers in an ancient land.

A Privileged Job

WHEN the job-seeker's representative asked me what qualifications I had for a job, I told her I had a master's degree.

'Don't put anything highfalutin' like that on your job sheet,' she told me. 'You're only going to end up a cleaner.'

I think of that sometimes when I'm scrubbing toilets in the middle of the night in my job as hospital aide in a small country hospital.

And if I ever need a reminder that this is a privileged job, I think of the young woman I was on shift with one night telling me, in the kitchen: 'One night my friends hassled me. They said, "You have to clean up shit." And they laughed at me. And I said, "Yes, I do. Because those people need someone to help them." And then they went quiet. And they haven't hassled me since.'

So that's what we do. We do things for people when they can't manage by themselves anymore. We shift a pillow under their head to help them sleep. We wheel them to the toilet when they can't walk, we do whatever needs to be done. We take their teeth out and clean them and put them back in in the morning. We feed them when they can't remember what a spoon is for. When they're dying, we make them whatever they feel like eating, even if it's custard or poached eggs for days in a row, until they can no longer swallow. We shave them, wipe their faces, pluck their chins, put their lipstick on. We remember how they like their tea and which socks are theirs. We remember who they were when they first came in and could tell us stories – of the Chinese miner up on Mt Buster, who lived in a tin hut on the slopes of the family farm and invited the farmhands to dinner one snowy day when they were mustering, and who threw pieces of gold out to children on the streets of Arrowtown.

We remember they had a little brown and white dog they loved, or a palomino quarter horse. They didn't always dribble. On the walls behind their beds are photos of their farms, the tussock and their beloved dogs. There are wedding photos, grandchildren photos. A man may seem odd, alone, without history, then suddenly tell you that this is the date on which his wife died ten years earlier, and how much he misses her.

What you begin to understand is that all this loss is ahead of you too – loss of your home, of your land, of your partner, loss of the most faithful dog you ever owned, loss of your garden, of your favourite tree. Loss of your memory, perhaps, of all these things.

We ask them about their lives, or we remind them. We play Brahms' *Hungarian Dances* to a woman who once taught music, and she smiles. We tell another how beautiful her fingers are and she tells us, 'I played the violin.'

It's the sort of job you do when you haven't got many options – when you didn't further your education, or you did and couldn't get a job. Or you chose to live somewhere where there are no jobs.

'You girls should get paid a thousand dollars a week for what you have to do,' one woman said as I cleaned her.

We get paid just over the minimum wage. We get paid for changing briefs, cleaning toilets, putting Steradent on teeth and pulling socks on misshapen feet. Being kind and remembering is the extra option.

Being kind is what reminds you of your humanness, your shared trajectory.

'I didn't think my life would come to this,' one man said as I guided him to the toilet. 'I thought I would just drop dead of a heart attack.' And sometimes they do, right in our arms. Those that don't are the ones we look out for. Thinking of our own fathers or mothers, living far away. Thinking of … thinking of what could be up ahead for each of us.

The Hawkdun Range

THE HAWKDUNS are the mountains I lift my eyes to – the long blocky length of them, butted up to Mt Ida at the head of the Ida Valley. From the valley their crest looks flat, and their sides bulge down in gullies and fissures to the valley floor. Tussock-covered and golden, the flanks catch the light of the setting sun and in the dawn are hazy blue, ephemeral.

At this point in my ecological education I don't know much. I struggle to remember yarrow, and the yellow potentilla. I don't know the breadth of plants in the high country, nor their names. The hills and rocky tors are what they mean to me when the sun sets and flings a brightness on the rocks. But what the hill is for itself I don't know, and this is the journey I wish to make: from the gaze to knowledge. From taking the pleasure of sight, the trickery of light, to giving the honour of attentiveness.

I think that because I have built with mud, my hands for days coated in the very material of this earth, that I too am of here, a part. But how little I know of this place where I live.

The farmers around me know this land historically: from patterns of weather stretching back decades, to which family lived where, which farm belonged to whom and then was lost, regrouped. Where boundaries began. Like me, they might not know the names or the existence of the smallest leafed beings.

American ecologist Charles Goodrich wrote, 'When people pay close attention to specific places, their study of place will reveal broad truths that go beyond that place … There is wisdom to be gained, for the more we know about the natural world and the place of humans in the world, the greater our insight into how we ought to live our lives.'

Not long into a walk with Graeme Male up the flank of the Hawkdun Range near Johnstones Creek, we see a sign warning of an 'unexploded ordnance', urging us to stay on the track for the next 100 metres or risk death or injury.

Humans having a say on the mountain. For 100 metres we stay on the track. Graeme stoops down.

'Here's some unexploded ordnance,' he says, holding up a live bullet, a slim, tapered ten-centimetre body. We discuss what to do with it. Graeme lays it just off the track.

'But what if a four-wheel drive vehicle comes up,' I say, 'and swerves at this point and runs over it? Would it go off?'

'It could if it was caught between the tyre and a sharp rock.'

'Throw it down the gully then.' Graeme lobs the bullet into the tussock. It lands silently.

(Later a local tells me they call Walking Spur, the path we're on, 'Unexploded Bomb Path', after the air force dropped six bombs in here on a training exercise in the 1960s and only recovered five.)

The track is rocky and suitable for four-wheel drives. On each side is an inhospitable mass of Spaniard grass, matagouri and tussock. The sky is blue and the sun warm enough after this morning's frost. We stop to take off merino layers. From across the hill the sound of a dog barking. Soon two vehicles come into view and begin to growl their way up the slope. The dog appears first, a large black one. It completely ignores us, so intent on its uphill rush. And then the four-wheel drives, family wagons with adults and children on board.

'Need a lift?' one driver asks.

'We're all good thanks.'

'You're missioning it,' he grins.

'Yep.' The children lean out of the back window waving at us. I think of the bullet tossed into the gully. The wagons reach the top and disappear. We start climbing again.

This morning Brian had left before me to go fishing for the day, heading out into the wild as we have. Graeme and I talk for a while about how one person's actions can inspire others. If you make a shift in yourself to do what you believe in, others around you may be freed to do the same.

Nearer the top we take an old steep track that leads to an outcrop of rocks. The tussock is shorter now, and Spaniard does not grow at this height. I turn off to walk between the tussocks on small trails over stones. Unlike the man-made track that funnelled us up the hillside, this is more like walking on the skin of the mountain. There's the feel and smell of the earth and the leaves. Asking the way forward, rather than taking it, assuming it.

There are small grey plants with fruit that look like white blueberries, one with red jewel-like berries, plants with tiny pink or white flowers, a bobbly coppery plant with small balls on long stems, a shrub with intricate foliage, and tough hebes (veronicas) with small orange flowers. I have a book at home, *Wild Central* by Neville Peat, and I've read chapters of it and not taken notes. I haven't retained the names of the plants. After I left university, prematurely, I took a job in a nursery repotting plants whose names have stayed with me for over forty years – *Choisya ternata*, *Albizia julibrissin*, *Cordyline australis*, *Ceanothus* … But I don't know the names of the plants on the mountains where I live. I walk through their beauty in a state of ignorance.

When I lived by the sea in Motueka, I didn't know the seabirds' names, not all of them. My enjoyment came from watching them, the long slow wading and dipping as they made their way along the tideline, the sea in small glassy ripples and the seabed puckered and dimpled by crustaceans. There was a smell of seaweed and salt, and the harsh call of a heron flapping in its ungainly way overhead. It wasn't until I wrote a book set mostly on that stretch of coast (*Fishing from the Boat Ramp: A guide to creating*) that I needed, at the editorial stage, to be correct in my bird names. Which birds were calling out in the early morning as they flew over the houses to feed in the fields?

A board down by the old wharf displayed drawings of the local birds with their names, and for the first time I could chant red-billed gull, black-backed gull, oyster catcher, pied stilt, bar-tailed godwit. My enjoyment of the birds had been tinged with ignorance. Now, knowing and naming each one as I watched it, white heron, black-fronted tern, was a way of acknowledging its uniqueness in this world. Not just something to look upon. As American conservationist Aldo Leopold put it, not 'a commodity' (for the gaze) but part of 'a community to which we belong'.

Not knowing the names of plants I walked among was part of the same ignorance I'd had for years on the beach. To know something, its shape and name and particularities, means to be aware of it consciously, and leads to a greater chance you'll want to protect it, to ensure it stays in this world, sharing the rights to clean air and space and water.

I began to think my walking among the plants was an infringement on their right to live un-stepped upon, and moved back to the stony path.

Scree slopes on the left now, instead of the richness of tussock and hebe and boulder. We pick our way over rocks so tumbled and deep on the track we could be walking a river uphill. The last haul up and we are on the top of the great rounded ridge of the Hawkduns. The rocks all about us are shattered, bouldered, shaled, shingled, strewn. The wind pushes and buffets us. The track leads away along the ridge, heading towards rocks and peaks, through stonefields and sparse tussock, into the distance where the highest peaks still have snow patches and clouds gather. The land swoops down on one side to the Maniototo, the Ida and the Manuherekia valleys, and on the other in a series of brown and rugged folds and spurs, dropping steeply to unknown valleys. Beyond us are mountain ridges and peaks, some of which Graeme has climbed.

We crouch behind tussocks to eat lunch, our backs to the wind. Brian told me a local story of a deep snowfall that came suddenly; of how the farmers had worried for the thousands of sheep up on the slopes. When they reached them the sheep were alive, safely sheltered under the big bunchy snow tussocks.

There have been other extreme snowfalls up here. In 2013 volunteers were helicoptered onto the slopes to tramp a path to safety for the sheep. There was a big one in 1895 too, but the worst was July 1908. Snow fell up to two and a half metres deep and lay on the ground in the valleys for seven weeks. In Naseby the people moved about in newly dug ditches, their heads and shoulders all that showed above the snow. Six kilometres this side of Rough Ridge, a honeymoon couple and ten others were trapped for a day and a night without food, water or warmth when their train ran into snow a metre and a half deep on the tracks. Clotheslines were buried at some homes, still with a full wash of linen and clothes beneath the frozen surface. The sheep suffered the most: the snow fell so fast and so thickly they were buried before the men could get to them. On some runs there were losses of forty percent.

'It was a week before any word came in from the outside world,' wrote the special reporter for the *Otago Witness*. 'From Wedderburn Station, for instance, there is nothing, as far as the eye can reach, but thousands of acres of dazzling whiteness, bounded by mountains … They stand around like the masterpieces of an Arctic god, their serrated edges gleaming against the sky …'

The clouds flock to us, and soon the valleys have vanished. The path is all we have – a boulder path, which means each footfall must be carefully chosen. Rain on my face, across my shoulders, on the fronts of my thighs. I have forgotten gloves because it's summer. My hands chill as I hold my jacket tight against the wind. Keep plodding.

Graeme slows to walk beside me, his jacket bright in a world of mist and rock.

'You know, everything you want is on the other side of fear,' he says. 'That's been my experience of living here.'

I think of how we both changed our lives. He and Donna shifted from Auckland, I from Motueka, to a valley we'd seen once, following some deep prompting of our hearts. And this is part of what we chose – this lonely track through mist. And then this, when the wind tears the clouds away so that the clumps of tussock are back, and the boulderfields with grey and green mosses, and then the slopes and the valleys before us again, the far peaks.

'We forget we're elemental,' says Graeme. 'Humans can imagine abstract concepts, like democracy. That's intangible, and yet it can have dominion over life. People die for it. When I was in the city I lived an intellectually understanding life, but now I'm leading a more elemental life. It exposes the fraudulent nature of a life where people are disconnected from the tangible.'

Bright sun again. We turn our faces to it.

Last month when I climbed neighbouring Mt Ida, I looked out at the valleys and hills and could only name them. Now, from the ridge on the Hawkduns, I see Blackstone Hill and North Rough Ridge and know those hills more intimately. I've walked along their ridges. I know the feel of the tors, warm and textured under my hand. I know of the tarns, and the small marshy hollows.

When we are far enough along the Hawkduns to see the Manuherekia River, I remember the tributaries I followed with Brian. I see the gully where Rocks Creek comes out, see the liquid silver of it running across the land towards the river. I remember the shags flying overhead, the small wild fish, and the clear clean water tumbling down the stones between the tussock grasses on the slopes of Mt St Bathans.

Otago Witness, 12 September 1895

I have the conviction that had the millions of snow tussocks been allowed
to grow in their wild state instead of being consumed by wilful fires, the
mortality in livestock would not have been so great in this and previous
winters, neither should we have suffered from drought to the extent we have
been doing of late years in Central Otago.

President of the Dunedin Chamber of Commerce, 1923

The insistent miner has scarred and scored every ravine and gully. The
rapacity of the sheep owner has burnt and eaten out the marvellous wealth
of native grass lands.

Professor Alan Mark, 2009

'[Tussock grassland] was important not only for biodiversity values but for
water, recreation and landscape reasons,' he said.

The production of water was a major issue and information he had got out
of research in the Te Papanui Conservation Park on the Lammerlaw and
Lammermoor ranges, west of Dunedin, showed the tussock landscape's
ability to produce water in its natural state was remarkable … 'It's a world
record in terms of vegetation.'

In the past people made mistakes through a lack of knowledge and
awareness of the consequences of their actions, such as the loss of forest,
of water, of plants, of birds. But what are we doing today that will have
consequences of loss or degradation? To even consider that question, a
person would need to look around with wider eyes. To look not just at
what has been done in their lifetime, or what they're being advised to do by
agencies they respect (and which may be acting for personal remuneration
or power), but to examine closely the interdependence of all that's around
them.

Many look back now with relief and understanding at those who
have taken a wider gaze, who have taken into consideration the
interconnectedness of all species and beings and said, 'Hold on …' Those
who were told they were 'standing in the way of progress'. Those who, for

example, prevented the level of Lake Manapōuri being raised; who halted development of a proposed aluminium smelter at the entrance to Otago Harbour close to the albatross colony; who stopped the damming of rivers like the Nevis and the Ahuriri (though the Ōhau was destroyed); who checked the desecration of the wild and rolling tussocked downs of the Lammermoors (though the Great Moss Swamp was lost to irrigation); and who are doing their best now to stop OMV prospecting for oil in the deep waters off the Otago coast, or the abuse of animals in slaughterhouses. And being called traitors for this, the way pacifists were once called traitors, were once locked up and decried: 'exploiter, shirker, weak-kneed quibbling, quaking conscientious objector and other such specimens,' in the words of Steve Boreham of Hawkdun Station in 1916.

People continue to burn tussock. And matagouri – whole hillsides of it one day along the road to Dunedin. First I saw the smoke from a multitude of fires rising into the blue sky, then came across the crackling orange flames and the charred, thorned branches – all in the name of grass.

In Nebraska, a local scientist told me, an organisation called the Conservation Reserve Enhancement Programme works with and pays farmers to take wetlands out of cropping and replant it in native grasses and trees. Its goals are:

> to significantly reduce the amount of irrigation water consumptive use and agricultural chemicals and sediment entering waters of the State from agricultural lands and transportation corridors. The reduction of ground and surface water use and of non-point (run-off from farmland) source contaminants, through establishment of permanent vegetative cover, will also enhance associated wildlife habitat, both terrestrial and aquatic. These goals are to be accomplished by terminating all irrigation practices on 100,000 acres [40,500ha] of land located in the State Conservation Priority Area for Water Quality.

Some 34,400 hectares are to be established in permanent native grasses, 4000 hectares in filter strips and riparian planting, and 2000 in wetland restoration.

The 2019 annual performance report of the Nebraska Platte-Republican Resources Area shows a reduction of 39,000 acre-feet (the amount of water needed to flood an acre one foot deep: 1233.3m^3) in water consumption, enhanced stream flows, and an enormous drop in the use of herbicide and fertiliser, which continues to improve water quality. An added benefit of not powering irrigation systems is the annual saving of over 8 million kilowatt-hours and over 2 million litres of fossil fuel. Groundcover plantings are successfully providing habitat for numerous species.

So far in New Zealand, there are no schemes to provide rental income to farmers who retire land along water corridors and other areas of significance to water quality. There needs to be. In the meantime, with our limited knowledge, what decisions will we make to conserve our limited supply of fresh water?

The night before I climb the Hawkduns a second time I ring Rachel Baxter, a volunteer with the Central Otago Ecological Trust (COET) and the Clyde Railhead Community Eco-Nursery. I want some pointers about the plants I am likely to see up there, and to ask if she ever collects seed in the Hawkduns.

'When I go into the mountains or high country, I like to look for plants I don't know,' she tells me. 'Ones I've never seen before. I probably won't collect seed from up on the Hawkduns for the nursery, as the weather in the Alexandra basin is so dry they wouldn't survive in the wild down here. I just want to see what's up there, and keep an eye on what's happening on the mountain.' She gives me a list of plants she noticed on her last trip: false Spaniard or *Celmisia lyallii*, the white-flowering *Veronica buchananii*, *Gentianella* and *Dracophyllum pronum*. She tells me to look up the website iNaturalist NZ, which I do. I study photos, take notes.

The day Brian and I climb Walking Spur into the Hawkduns is the day before the smoke from the Australian bushfires, already travelling across the ocean, rolls over our valley and smudges out even the Home Hills and Rough Ridge across the paddock. The sky turns a surreal and weirdly threatening yellow/grey, bringing something of the fear of destruction in its whiff. But today we don't know that's coming, and we take for granted our own and our country's safety, the blue sky, the far vision, the mountains that are revealed to us as we climb: the Hectors, the Remarkables behind us, the white peak of Tititea/Mt Aspiring to the left. When we reach the rounded stony crest of the Hawkduns, there in the far distance is Aoraki/Mt Cook, the highest mountain in New Zealand. Long Spur folds away from us at a right angle, and to our right is Mt Ida and, beyond that, Mt Buster, Mt Kyeburn, Mt Dommet and St Marys Range.

On the highest point of Mt Ida there's a cairn, and buried beneath the top stone is a small jar with notes, paper and pen. At 1690 metres you can sit and read messages going back decades that have been folded and left in the jar. On another trip up there I scribbled a poem and added it to notes that spoke of rain and mist, views and good times with friends.

On the way up the Hawkduns my eyes are for the plants. It's early summer and the alpine plants are blooming. On the lower slopes the introduced hieraceum sports raggy yellow blooms like dandelions between the tussocks. Higher up, it's evident that the native flora and fauna are free to grow unaffected by intensive agricultural processes.

As a result of a process of tenure review, much of our alpine country is now protected as public conservation land: the Hawkduns themselves form part of the 65,000-hectare Oteake Conservation Park, opened in 2010. The park covers mountainous high country, tussock plateaus, scree slopes, shrubland and wetlands. Early iwi hunted weka and gathered plants here. On a lower slope near Little Bremner Creek is the site of an ancient tool-making quarry where porcellanite was worked.

Brian strides ahead, and I keep stooping and looking, taking photos, trying to name plants. There's the narrow-leafed snow tussock, of course, *Chionochloa rigida*, and false Spaniard – which at first I take for a yellow flowering daisy. I find small shrubs of hebes on patches of stones and growing out of banks, their thin clamped branches opening into flowers. I call Brian back to look at a weird upright broom. The sun has lifted over the mountain top and lights up the plant, its bare poky branches thickly clustered with flowerheads that look like white boysenberries. The branches are grooved, a yellow-green colour, and so random in their direction that the plant looks like something Dr Seuss might have drawn, as one person describes it. It's *Carmichaelia crassicaulis*, coral broom, and an endangered species. A little higher along the track there's a shrub with upright needled leaves about twenty-five centimetres long, thin branches marked with rings and the leaves shaded in colour from green to orange to brown. A *Dracophyllum longifolium* or inaka, iNaturalist tells me. These shrubs can live for over 200 years; maybe this very plant survived the 1908 snowfall. Now I know what Rachel means about that joy of finding and being able to name something you've never seen before.

A skink crosses our path. It's larger, sturdier, darker than the ones we've seen flicking through the tussock and between the stones. We wonder if it could be one of the rare species – the Grand or the Otago skink? My camera is zipped in my backpack. We have only a few seconds to track it with our eyes and commit it to our memory.

When I message Grant Norbury, senior scientist and trustee of COET, he replies: 'Unlikely to be Grand or Otago but could have been a Lakes skink from the green skink complex.'

COET was formed fifteen years ago by Alexandra residents keen on wildlife conservation and community participation. The trust's vision is to bring back the critically endangered lizards that have been vanishing as their dryland homes disappear. At the trust's Mokomoko Dryland Sanctuary, a fourteen-hectare fenced dryland habitat, the native vegetation is beginning to thrive again. Within it, endangered skinks and geckos are introduced, monitored and protected.

On the top of the Hawkduns Brian and I look out over the cleft of our valley between the two long, parallel block ranges of Rough Ridge and Blackstone Hill.

'What amazes me,' my friend Evelyn had said, 'is that once this was all under the sea.'

That was round about 23 million years ago. From 19 to 16 million years ago Lake Manuherekia stretched as far as our eyes can see. I recently read, in Hamish Campbell and Gerard Hutching's *In Search of Ancient New Zealand*, that geologists have long been interested in the sediments from this lake because the deposits are coal-bearing and have been actively mined in places such as the Ida Valley. Finally, I'd found where the coal was from that kept appearing on the banks of my stream. Coal millions of years old.

We sit out of the wind beside a large structure of rock, so lichen-covered and textured it could be barnacled, a 'dried-out submarine seascape' as Campbell and Hutching wrote of rocks on the Chatham Islands. The 'shore' by our feet is the soft rounded humps of raoulia growing on the rocks, and green moss. In all the silence, a bird begins to trill. The sound comes from nowhere and everywhere. It's a skylark, 'bouncing on air'.

'What I hope, when I'm up in wild places like this,' Brian says, 'is that I'll return home with my perspective altered.'

My heart is enlarged by crassifolia, by inaka, by a quick, black skink.

'To be more respectful,' Brian says. 'And more at peace, too.'

In early spring I'd joined those protesting at the Petroleum Conference in Queenstown; thirty-five of us, with our Climate Emergency tape wrapped around the perimeter of the Millennium Hotel hosting the delegates. When a security guard pulled me away from the hotel, I said to him, 'We're doing this for you, too. And for your children.'

'I know,' he said. But stood there still, with police; so many police and guards that at times they outnumbered us.

My granddaughters Indy, Lacey and Scarlett joined me for a while on the kerb holding their signs:

> **Business As Usual** and **Stop Burning**
> **Is Over** **Our Future**

It didn't stop a bus driver swerving his vehicle at us as he yelled, 'Fuck you!'

We were grandmothers, students, teachers, builders – my son-in-law Sam Deavoll, with one of his apprentices …

'Get a bloody job!' another motorist yelled.

'I'm on my holiday!' yelled back protestor Jack Brazil.

An electrician in a van with his company name bold on the side pulled the fingers and yelled at me.

This is my wider community, the town where my grandchildren are growing up.

But there were others who waved and honked support over those six hours.

When the petroleum delegates broke for lunch, some stood in a group staring down at us from the second-storey hotel window. I held up my sign:

> **What will YOU do**
> **to protect**
> **our EARTH?**

One man looked straight at me and I stared back, hands clenched on my pole. Half a minute went by. Then he smiled. Some sort of wry smile. Enough to say, I see you. I smiled back at him. For a moment it was as if the walls between us had melted.

Both human. One shared earth.

'The way forward is not simply a matter of urging our government to show more leadership,' says Catherine Knight in *Beyond Manapouri*:

> Such demands will simply be counteracted by those whose interests are served better by the status quo. For New Zealand to respond to the environmental issues we face, I believe something much more fundamental is required – that is, a cultural shift in the way we think about the environment and our responsibilities towards it.

On the Hawkduns the land is left to nature. (Some farmers, like Barry Becker, believe the land would do better with light grazing, 'to try to control the weed problems that have either happened already or will eventually,' he is quoted as saying in Brian Turner's book *Boundaries*.) The rest – the lowlands, and the remnants of wetlands, salt pans and areas where threatened plants and creatures live – is mostly in private ownership. In many places the soil is under threat. 'I believe we've almost poisoned our soil,' Barry says in *Boundaries*. 'Much of the biodiversity's gone. We're going to have to try and correct that.'

What we need, Knight suggests, is an integrated system, one where land is productive *and* conserved, avoiding the polarised positions created by nature/agribusiness. 'In Germany for instance,' she says, 'a forest that is grown to produce timber is also utilized at all times of [the] year by hunters, bikers and hikers as well as being a fully functioning ecosystem that supports a diverse web of diversity.'

How do we begin to move towards this? I think of Aldo Leopold's 'Land Ethic': 'We can be ethical only in relation to something we can see, feel, understand, love, or otherwise have faith in.'

Shadows form in my mudbrick writing studio. It's 9.30pm, the sky darkening outside. Yet something calls, and I put on my gumboots and jacket and go outside. There is mist among the tors on Rough Ridge and a bright banner of red in the southwest sky. I walk into the long meadow grass where small moths cloud at every footstep as if they are accompanying me. Beyond the willows frogs croak. I head towards the stream, where I haven't been for weeks. The stones are pale in the twilight, seeming to give off their own light. I watch the silvery clattery water, a good wide flow for summer. And when I turn my head to the wide flood-stripped area, what was once bare stones, coal deposits and the remnants of torn-out broom has been transformed by wildflowers. They have grown among the stones as if this were meadow too: white yarrow, cobalt viper's bugloss, woolly mullein with yellow buds (once called 'witches taper'). There are purple and white clovers, yellow-flowering St John's wort, and the high white flowers of oxeye daisies. I walk among them, my fingers reaching out to them. There's no thistle or gorse or broom or any other plant that would engender lists of things to do. Instead it is the short-term wonder of flowers that bloom here under the soft, greying sky. I'm glad to be alone with the moths and frogs, the light on water and the stillness of the air; everything hushed.

Where the stream blocks my way, I climb the bank and walk across the paddock to the broom forest where I planted seedling kōwhai trees in autumn. I crouch into the tunnel of broom with my torch on.

The kōwhai trees are thriving. Sheltered from snow and scorching winds they've grown inches, their branches spidery with dainty leaves. There are no wild pigs here, none of the cattle who made these tunnels. I follow the dark pathways through the broom past kōwhai after kōwhai shining in my torchlight: hidden and secret and alive.

A Roof Over Our Heads

SAM AND I were on site when the sun came up. We stopped unloading tools from the van and turned to watch Blackstone Hill light up orange and pink. After three months of building we knew how fleeting the light changes were: Mt Ida translucent in early dawn, late-afternoon gilded light on Rough Ridge, and then at the end of the day, on a good day, the Hawkduns and the Ida Range pink as well, a showcase of folds and ridges before dark and starlight appeared.

A few days earlier Sam had said to me, 'You have no idea how much we have to do before the straw bales go in, do you?'

I shook my head. It was Sam who held the enormity of everything we had to do in his head. And the urgent task in front of us now was the roof.

'Well, lack of knowledge is a wonderful thing,' he said. 'You just keep on as you are; stay positive.'

And I did. Every day I pictured the house with the roof on, the bales safely in before winter, even a bench outside in the sun.

Mid-morning, Sam set me up on the grass to cut, fold and roll the building paper that would go under the iron. I rolled the heavy tarpaper over the bumpy ground, measured, cut, then bent and creased a strip on each side to make a channel for any moisture to run safely away instead of getting into the ceiling. I curled each folded piece into a loose black roll and stacked them beside me.

When he was an apprentice Sam didn't like doing this job, but I enjoyed it. I liked working on the ground after what seemed like weeks of being up on the beams and joists. I was warm in the sun, and birds sang in the willows as my fingers smoothed and pressed the paper. For once I had a familiar task, as if the rolls were curtains I hemmed and sewed.

When the first creased rolls were ready, I passed four to Sam and climbed the ladder to join him.

'Get ready to catch the paper as soon as it comes near you,' he called from the apex of the roof. 'If the wind catches it, it'll rip, and we haven't got paper to waste. Ready?'

'Yep.' I tightened my legs to balance on the lower part of the roof, hands held apart. He let the roll of building paper go and it uncurled in a rush towards me. The wind snatched at the paper before I grabbed it. I hung onto one corner.

'Hold it down!' called Sam. 'Lean across it, don't let it rip!' He climbed down the rafters to me, then made his way up, stapling the paper until he was at the top again. 'Okay, next one. Ready?'

'Yep.'

When we had one quarter of the first part of the roof covered in black paper, Sam came down and showed me how to carry the long lengths of red roofing iron over to the building so I could prop them up before lifting them, hand over hand, to where he could grab them.

'Think you can carry them?' he checked.

'Sure.' The lengths of iron were heavy and cut into my gloves. I had to hold the sheets in the middle so they didn't buckle and crease. I pushed them up to Sam and he carried them the rest of the way by himself, stepping confidently up the rafters, the concrete floor exposed below him. Any weight or discomfort I felt on the ground was nothing compared to carrying the sheets while stepping on rafters. What daring, what perseverance a roofer needed to have.

A builder needs to be courageous, for sure. Strong, in order to move the heavy building materials. Forward-thinking, for all the planning that has to go on. A lateral thinker and problem solver, because, as my sometime building mate Brian Turner would quote to me, 'Nothing succeeds as planned.' So far, we were doing well.

I said to Sam, 'Does it make things harder having your mother-in-law as your worker?'

'You're better than most young apprentices,' he said, 'because you understand that you don't know the building process. When I tell you to do a job, you do it, and when I show you how to do a task, you listen. You haven't brought any ego or bravado to the site.'

That made up for something. And I did make sure I was biddable. I would stop doing my job to get tools for Sam when he asked. I'd throw them accurately to the roof, keeping my eye on Sam and following through so he could catch them easily. I appreciated the way he worked hard and fast, at the same time coaching me along. I know he wished at times that he had another builder who could take the brunt of some of the work, but even if there was a spare builder around these parts, I was way past being able to afford another paid helper.

When we first started building, Sam would arrive on Tuesday mornings and work through to Friday afternoons. Now, with the pressures of bale-raising day and winter fast approaching, he made the decision to stay on site. We had to get the roof on so the bales could go in and the mud plaster on before frosts came. That meant working every day without a break.

With the roof, we began work while it was still dark and stayed on site after the sun set until we could no longer see. Then we'd lock the tools in the van and go in and light candles in the caravan. Dinners became as easy as we could make them. Cans of tomatoes heated up with any vegetables we had. Rice, or pasta. No hot bath to relax in. It was eat and sleep, Sam in the caravan and I by torchlight in a small tent under the willows.

In the dark of morning we ate fruit and drank coffee in the caravan while we talked through the tasks of the day. Sam made lists of materials by candlelight. Then out by the work van I cajoled my body to get moving – arms above my head and leaning back to stretch. Buckling on the toolbelt was a sign: here we go again. With the sky lightening in the east and the radio on, another day's hard work seemed possible.

From the roof we had a good view of the road, the café, the traffic and the locals. Up there in the sun with our music on it felt like the best job in the world. Sheet by sheet the roof began to sheathe the house, creating shade for us below in the thirty- to forty-degree heat.

We knew some of the vehicles that went past, and amused ourselves by calling out to the drivers even though they couldn't hear us.

'Hey, Shazza!' Sam called to Sharyn McKnight, who passed us twice a day driving the school bus. We recognised Barry Becker's farm truck and waved and called, 'Hey, Barry!', though he kept his eyes on the road. If any stock were being driven down the main street of Ōtūrehua, Sam would call 'Traffic jam!' We'd watch the mob of sheep bobbing along the road, filling the whole width of it, clattering past the café and sometimes into the gardens if the dogs didn't get onto them fast enough. Or there'd be cattle, brown and white beasts trotting through the village. We'd stand on the roof, hammers in hand, and watch them.

On the third day of roofing we woke to a gusting wind. We'd been blessed with good weather so far. Days and days of hot, still weather. If there'd been rain, Sam wouldn't have been able to stand on the steep-pitched slopes, and wind would have prevented me from rolling out the paper to fold it. Now, with all the paper creased and in rolls, we made the decision to keep on working and finish putting the sheets on the roof.

One roll of building paper Sam sent down to me was hurled sideways by the wind before I could catch it. I grabbed and held on while it bucked and flapped in the wind. The edges began to tear. Sam struggled to hold his end down.

'It's going, let it go!' he called. The heavy paper ripped out of my hands and ended up in a mess in the paddock. I climbed down to bring more iron over.

The wind lifted and tugged at each long sheet as I staggered beneath. Along the road the power lines surged up and down. Even the toetoe was bent over by the wind. I pushed my gloved hands under another sheet and hoisted it. The wind shoved me sideways.

'Are you all right?' Sam yelled.

'Yes! 'I shouted back. The iron was worse than the paper, curving and pulling at our hands so that both of us fought to stay upright, but we managed to get one more sheet of iron on to protect the paper. Sam nailed it in place before calling time. The roof would have to wait.

In my old life, Dave and I built a hut on his land in the northwest Nelson ranges. The hut was my first experience of building. Although I didn't get to do any hammering or roofing, I sanded and primed and painted and helped mill the timber. I also kept the workers fed.

Up there on Pukeone/Mt Campbell, 900 metres above sea level, everything was prepared over a fire outside: roasts cooked in a camp oven, bread and damper baked over coals, a kettle suspended from a timber frame for the never-ending cups of coffee and tea. We slept in a small tent beside the fire. I bathed Evie, then a toddler, in an orange plastic tub in water warmed on the fire. At night we sat on logs and ate from plates on our knees. Kea circled in the dusk and called out their lonely cries. The sky filled up with stars.

We milled the dead standing timbers, and lugged the beams out of the forest between us on our shoulders. Evie dawdled on the track in front of us. We emerged blinking out of the bush onto the bright slopes of mountain grass. We left the world of elegant, ancient trees and mossy boulders and stepped into the world earlier settlers had created, where toppled beech trees lay burnt among the boulders. We had to pick our way over and between the trunks blackened by fire, their texture roughened and grey as if they were driftwood tossed up on some remote shore.

And that very mountain *had* been a shore. Trilobites, brachiopods and shell beds help to date the rocks to 60 million years ago; slopes heaved up from the ocean in some cataclysmic birthing of the land, the shoreline in one life uplifted to be ridges and folds of rock in another. Transformation on a tectonic scale.

To the Roman author Vitruvius, an engineer and architect in the first century BC, the hut was the beginning of all architecture. The simplicity of those first primitive huts, constructed from and imitating nature, is something we as humans still yearn for, says Joseph Rykwert, an architectural historian. They remind us of a time when 'man was quite at home in his house, and his houses as right as nature itself'.

Dave and I didn't know anything then about Vitruvius or the concept of the primitive hut, only that we needed to build something for shelter out of what was around us up there on the mountain. Yet the instinct of a structure that mimicked nature – four upright trees and a canopy of branches – still guided us.

Inside, the walls were bare of any lining. The floor we made from planks of tōtara and beech. We nailed silver insulation under the floor, but a few hours later a wind came tearing out of the west and ripped it to shreds. After that the floormats would levitate in strong gusts of wind. We held them down with chunks of firewood.

When it snowed with a wind like that, the snow forced its way through the gaps between the window frames and landed on the kitchen bench. Yet the hut was small enough to be warm if we kept the fire going throughout the day and night. Firewood lay abundant on the hillside.

Our hut was much like the first homes built by pioneers. They too used whatever materials were to hand and had no electricity, just a need for shelter. I liked to look up at the ceiling at night, at the planks and beams, knowing that however uneven they were, we had milled them all. And it was comforting to live in one room with a bed and a fire, with windows above the dining table that looked out on a white world. This world we were sheltered in was sufficient unto our needs.

At the old Golden Progress quartz mine, along the road from me here in Central Otago in a narrow valley made icy in winter, a noticeboard displays a copy of a letter from one J.H. Watmuff, a miner who had camped on Rough Ridge in a canvas tent with a broken arm. Overnight the rain seeped into his bedding, and in the morning a foot of snow chilled the air. 'The coldest most miserable night of my life', he called it.

When Dave and I were camping by the cooking fire up on Pukeone we'd say to each other, 'Won't it be great when the hut is built.' Soon we'd have a house; we could cook inside, we could sleep out of the wind. But when the hut was finished and we moved in, we found the wood and iron structure separated us from living close to the land. We no longer cooked outside or sat out there to eat with the kea and the stars. We didn't lie on the ground to sleep, or feel the drama of the wind. Even in that simple hut we missed the pleasure of living in the environment.

We desire shelter, protection from the elements. But a shelter can stifle our awareness of where we live – the sky, the terrain, the weather, the plants, animals and birds that live alongside us in our own place. Our *place* – that something that watches over us, lasts beyond us and participates in our moments.

The first night I stayed in my finished strawbale house, here in the Ida, I lit the fire and sat and looked at the walls around me. It was different from any house I'd ever been in. I looked at the candlelight flickering on the mud walls textured with straw. The handprints of those who had helped to build the house still showed in the final coat.

I knew then what was different. In this house the walls are made from the very material of the earth. Mud walls surrounded me, and as the firelight and candle flames flickered over them, creating small shadows and gleams of light, I had the distinct feeling of being inside a living, breathing structure. Instead of feeling cut off from the earth, I felt I was being held by the earth, taken care of by the earth. The house was quiet, still, warm.

But long before that, before the straw went in and while the roof was still open to the sky, people began to arrive for the strawbale-raising day.

My friend Bridget Auchmuty was the first, a fellow writer all the way from Nelson. I took my toolbelt off and left Sam nailing ply, and went with Bridget across the paddock to help her pitch her tent. We held the flapping ends and wrestled her shelter up, then turned to watch the hills. The sun, setting low in the west, threw a golden light onto Rough Ridge, lighting the rocky tors in relief. Long grass rippled away from us, as golden as the tussock on the hill.

'Is that Sam yelling?' Bridget asked.

We looked across to the unfinished house in the distance and there was Sam gesturing, up on the roof, the sky paling behind him.

'What?' I yelled back, and started running towards him.

'The wind,' he yelled. 'It's dropping! We can finish the roof!'

Cycling with Bartali: A year in the valley

Snow

Just out of the village the road is torn up by the recent flood. Snow is piled along the roadside. Last week the Ida Burn flowed from one side of the road to the other. There are logs jammed in the fence lines, tangled dead grass and sticks. Only the stalks and flowerheads of yarrow stand up straight from the grass.

Bartali whirs ahead. He is the one who seriously wants to get fit and compete. He's been close several times in the nationals; he still has something he wants to achieve. What do I want? To keep up would be good. To be fit enough for the long roads of exploration. When I'm unfit, like today, he tells me to ride in his lee. Even here, the wind still catches and is like frost on my face.

Not far from the village the snow has gone. The paddocks are brown, the grass cropped short and soaked from the flood. There are hollows full of water. Dirty-fleeced sheep in a bare paddock, the earth dark and wet, the sheep at the edge of a newly opened section of fodder beet. They're the only stock to be seen in this whole stretch of the valley or on the slopes of Rough Ridge.

We climb one hill by the dam and, further down the straights into a head wind, another sharp hill. A gap opens up between Bartali and me and several times he has to call out 'Are you there?', and then cranes his neck back when he doesn't hear me close behind him.

'I'm coming,' I call, and press down harder on the pedals to catch up. We decide to turn not long after the second hill. I turn first, and then because Bartali doesn't catch up immediately, I put the bike in top gear and pedal flat out down the hill. The wind is behind me and for a few moments I feel capable of anything. When Bartali catches up, calling out that I burned him off, he maintains the pace. My exuberance used up, I settle in doggedly to keep up with him. It reminds me of how cycling (like life, writing, building, love …) mostly is for me: moments of illumination and deep joy and the rest, keeping at it as best you can.

When we pass the sheep again, the air is full of the turnipy smell of beets. In the village there are sandbags outside the first houses and snow piled up in the gutters and on the footpath. The Hawkduns are whiter than I've seen them, rich with snow. A weak sun lights their flanks.

At Bartali's gate I've had enough. He carries on up the valley a while. On his lawn I remember to pull my foot sideways out of the pedal so as not to fall on my side under his clothesline, the way I have before. This expertise at least I have retained.

Flood

Less than three hours of sleep after nightshift and the phone rings.

'Do you want to come out on the bike for half an hour?'

'I thought you've already been on the bike?'

'I've come back to see if you want to come out.'

Hard to say no to that dedication. Even without sleep.

'Okay, I'll come – on my mountain bike.'

We take the gravel road towards the Ida Valley station. Here the surface is badly damaged – rutted, deep with mud and with water still across the road in places. As I navigate a track as best I can, I think how it must have been for cyclists in Christchurch after the earthquakes, the roads buckled and fractured. How much for granted I have taken smooth roads.

Bartali leads me further and further from the tarseal road.

'Remember the bridge is taken out on Hills Creek Road,' I call out.

'We'll get across. The stream's gone down now.'

'How do you know? There's a big hole in the road.'

'Do you want to risk it?' he asks. And then because it's my favourite ride, round the back block, and I don't like turning back, I say yep, let's do it.

Way past the 'half hour' stage there's a sharp hill in the distance. I'm already dreading it.

'Are you there?' Bartali calls.

'Yes, I'm coming,' I call back, and push myself to catch up again.

'Make sure your bike is in the lowest gear before you start going up,' Bartali tells me. And after that it's pure grinding. In my lowly state I picture George Bennett on the Tour de France. Dig in, dig in. And when I crest the hill and finally look up, there's a long line of fog creeping in across the low hills. Above them the Hawkduns are luminous and lovely with snow.

I think of how far we have come, how cold it is, how close the fog is, and how far we will have to bike back if the road is impassable.

This side of the valley must be where all the stock are for now. There's a herd of black and white cattle grazing one paddock, another herd of shaggy, stumpy-legged Highland cattle across the road, and sheep as far as the eye can see. On Hamish's lake there are so many birds. Bartali and I don't have our glasses and can't tell what they are – paradise ducks for sure, and maybe Canadian geese and even swans. The long surface of the water speckled with them.

The road tilts down and now we're flying. The gravel surface sogged and dimpled with water. At speed and without glasses, I rely on guesswork to pick out a line. And in front is the bridge with the road taken out.

It's not until we get up close that we see the Ida Burn, though high and muddy, is back within its banks. And the hole in the road is just passable. Bartali lifts our bikes above his head onto the bridge and pulls me up.

Sun

A fine warm day for this time in winter, and the tussocks in my garden beginning to stir with the breeze. In the tawny paddocks the sheep are backlit, as if they're in a surreal painting, light along their backs. The Hawkduns, too, are becoming planes of shining white.

A few years back I took a six-week painting class in Cromwell with artist Megan Huffadine. Each day when I left class and drove back through the gorge, I'd see everything in terms of paint colour and brush stroke. The sensation would fade after a few hours. Being on the bike is a chance to bring back some of that attentiveness to the land around me. Close to the ground, it's easy to assimilate sights and sounds and smells, the feel of the wind, the lift and curve of the road.

From the corner of the Ida Valley I have to bike right behind Bartali's wheel to get any relief from the wind. With the climb and the wind, that means making moment-to-moment adjustments to keep us both safe. It's exactly the type of brain work I hope helps guard against dementia. And using thigh strength helps too. I read that somewhere.

Bartali gradually pulls ahead. I don't call out but plug on, slower now that I don't have his shelter. The wind blows directly in my face, bringing a sweet earth smell reminiscent of molasses. It takes a few moments to work out where it's coming from. Silage. Not that there are sheep in these paddocks by the road, but somewhere around here a farmer has fed out to the stock and there are traces still in the air.

The gap between Bartali and me opens up. He's way up the road before he realises I'm not on his tail anymore, and slows down.

'You have to call out,' he tells me when I catch up. 'If you get a wheel behind in this wind, you're gone out the back.'

'I was gone, just like that,' I say. And for a while, as we continue cycling into the wind, he calls out, 'Are you there?' 'Yes.' 'Are you there?' 'Yes.' 'Are you there?' 'Yes.' It reminds me of three-year-old grandson Sonny this morning, when he was walking with me to the shop: 'Are we there yet?' he asked, even though we hadn't reached the end of my drive.

Bartali and I turn at the stone house beyond Lockharts Hill. I'll know I'm fitter when I want to go beyond there, further towards St Bathans.

On the ride home Bartali calls out now and then, 'Are you still hanging in there?'

'Yes!' I call back.

It's our ritual, when we approach the village, to race through it. In summer there's a traffic sign that lets us know how fast we're going – 38, 40kmh – but in winter we speed up anyway. Bartali stands up on his pedals and takes off. It's so preposterous to me, his turn of speed and my state of exhaustion, that I laugh and don't even attempt to keep up. When he circles back to me, I say, 'You've got another whole super-gear.'

'I wish that was true,' he says. 'The trouble is, I compare myself to what I used to be capable of. I used to be strong on the hills, and a middling-good sprinter. It was a good combination. But I'm seventy-five now. Those days have gone.'

Will they even begin for me, now I'm over sixty? Who knows? It's a hot bath I'm thinking of right now. And a cup of tea.

Sunset

It's a fine line – to exercise or not. Outside, the sun lowering, the bank of clouds dulling the light, the day almost over. Yet at the computer, with such dullness and lethargy inside, it seems a bike ride is the only cure. I don't ring Bartali. If we go together it's a much tougher ride and I'm so close to not going. *Just take the mountain bike and ride twenty minutes up the rail trail and back again*, I tell myself. In the same way when I'm avoiding writing a scene. *Just write for ten minutes*, I coax myself – and often put down the pen to find forty minutes have passed.

It's after 4.30, the air cooling, and no-one else on the rail trail. The gravel road leads flat and straight into the distance. Sometimes farmers shift sheep along it, or locals walk their dogs. I push on the pedals, every turn an effort. How unmotivated I am, how unambitious – even slovenly – I feel. I make myself do a minute of fast riding to get my heart rate up. There's no enjoyment in the effort. I look at the apple trees instead.

Apple trees have grown up beside the railway line where once people threw cores out of the train windows. In summer the trees provide welcome fruit for cyclists on the rail trail, an abundance of spray-free heritage fruit. Two trees I pass still have garlands of yellow fruit hanging on, and sparrows jounce around in the bare branches. In all this bare-twig winterness, to see the trees like apple-lit fairy trees is to see the resoluteness of nature.

On Reef Road the section that was scoured out by flood has been repaired. There are cars on the main road across the paddock, but here on the trail I'm safe. No trucks coming too close to me, no cars overtaking as another approaches. There's a freedom to riding like this, with the whole wide trail on which to choose my own track.

Near the corner of the main road the track lifts, a gradual train-able rise. I begin to appreciate what's around me: the sabled flanks of Mt St Bathans, the white Hawkduns up ahead, the woolly flock of wethers grazing the tawny grass and grey matagouri. I stop at a small bridge and wait a while for the sun to come out for a photo. The stream burbles – still rushy with water and the banks of grass flattened in a wide channel from the flood. Birds in the bare willow singing, and in front of me it's all downhill back to the village.

I'm in top gear, speeding, no worries about trucks or potholes. How fast I am, swooping between fields, past sheep and the paddocks with new gravel seams. At last the sun drops below the cloud, blazes a brightness across the valley, lights up the rocky tors on Rough Ridge and gives an orange warmth to the bare poplars. It's what makes riding near sunset so spectacular.

On the way home I call in at Graeme and Donna's to check their flood repairs. There's a new bund in the driveway, new gravel. Inside, the carpet is re-laid and dry, the fire burning willow. Outside, Mt St Bathans in the last of the sun.

Distance

Snow is forecast down to 600 metres this afternoon. We're at 540 metres, so the hills around the valley will most likely get a good dusting. In preparation I put on woollen tights, extra socks, two shirts, two jackets, two pairs of gloves. There's a slight breeze, but nothing like the northwest gale of last night. I woke up this morning to find my verandah chairs upended in various places on the lawn, joined by the rake, the broom and one gumboot.

Bartali left earlier than me to cycle, and as I head up the valley with no sight of him I wonder if I listened to his instructions properly – up the valley or down the valley, or was he already up and back and I'd missed him? I chug on, the bike seeming to move effortlessly compared to the last outing. Have I become fit that quickly? For a few minutes I bask in the wonder of this, until I realise that northwest wind is on my tail. Like the way luck, or the opportunities you're born into, can make the road ahead so much easier.

Ah, but here's Bartali, swooping up over the bridge ahead and slowing down to join me.

I remember to say my cyclist's prayer. *May I be blessed and protected and my bike too* (that's to cover various contingencies like turning in gravel and forgetting to pull my foot out before the bike slides over, or in case heavy trucks or speeding cars come too close), then one for Bartali and his bike (to cover such things as me running into the back of his wheel) and for all people, traffic and creatures around us (to cover low-flying hawks, straying sheep and the aforementioned trucks and overtaking cars).

Bartali turns right at the T-intersection at the top of the valley. First, the hills. Or 'gnarly little bastards', as Bartali calls them. 'Though what I like about this ride,' he says, 'is that it's always a good measure of your fitness. You go in front and set the pace.' I move up, already starting to huff like a train.

At the top he tells me again, 'You need to change into your lowest chain ring when you're still part way up your sprockets. Don't leave it till you're in the lowest sprocket and still in your middle gear. It's too big an angle. You could throw your derailleur into your spokes.'

On the next hill I take his advice. It's a good feeling going confidently into that low gear. I feel like I've got some control over the situation.

In a long paddock sloping up towards the Hawkduns, sheep have their heads down eating hay that's spread in a circle. Hay, not silage, for there's no sharp tang in the air. Everywhere the paddocks are cropped short, tawny and slick after frosts and ice. The sheep don't even lift their heads to consider us. Across the road there's nothing happening at Becker's woolshed, though Barry has passed us three times in his truck, a black and white dog on the back running from side to side as if there's an exciting job coming up the moment he can leap off the deck.

We pass Wedderburn and, instead of turning back, Bartali heads on towards one of the steepest hills in the district. My nemesis.

'Go into your low gear about a third of the way up,' he calls back. It's a long, slow grind. I start wishing I'd done yoga breathing exercises for the past year. Anything that would help my ribs expand so my lungs don't feel like they are imprisoned by bone.

On the long, joyous downhill ride home, the sun breaks through the leaden clouds over the Dunstans. I stay in Bartali's lee and keep up my speed by concentrating on the distance between our wheels. The sun shines on his wheel rim and the heels of his cycling shoes. We charge into the village. The speed panel is up – 33kmh we're doing, and a ride of an hour and twenty minutes.

My old shoes are hanging in a bag on my gatepost, ready for the walk with the bike through the snow-slushy paddock to home. Bartali rides on up the street.

'Good riding!' he calls back to me.

Blue skies

This morning the frost was so severe the pond froze. Small birds skittered on the surface and the resident paradise ducks were out pecking in the frozen grass. It's warm in the sun on the verandah and, lulled by that, I head off for a bike ride minus the second jacket, second pair of gloves and newspaper down my front. The air is icy from last night's snow and a cold head wind as we lead down the valley.

'Get in behind,' Bartali calls out as we go through the village, startling the shopkeeper, John, who is out on the footpath.

The sky is blue and everything bright after days of cloud.

'Just look at that snow back on the Old Man Range,' Bartali says. The ranges shimmer in the distance, and I can imagine the Hector Mountains and the back of the Remarkables, seen from further down the valley, with their white peaks as well. 'And look at that snowmelt in the Ida.' The stream surges bank to bank under the bridge we're riding over.

We head up the first hill and I'm determined to keep up.

'You're a dogged bastard with your speed,' I say.

'I'm riding doggedly,' Bartali says. 'And I've got two voices in my head. One says *button off*, and the other says *keep it up, don't be a wuss*. I want to get better.'

Same. There are logs still jammed in the fence lines from the floods, and further up the sheep are still munching their way through the paddock of fodder beet. They've got half of the twelve-hectare paddock to go. No smell of beet as we ride past: the wind is swinging from the west.

The sheep, and two mares with their yearling foals in a far paddock, are the only stock for miles around. Such lovely, empty country.

The farmers are gearing up for spring though – Jimmy drives through a gateway with a long boom across his tractor, and further down the road equipment for ploughing waits by the fence line.

When we turn to go home Bartali picks up speed. 'Brace yourself,' he says, and I know there'll be suffering involved.

I can't think of anything good to say about thirteen kilometres of steadily rising road. Later Bartali tells me he kept up the pace by telling himself *just keep pedalling in circles, keep going …*

I plug on, sometimes lifting mine eyes to the mountains to remind myself why I am out here. The sun lights the long grass on the edge of the road as if it is tussock or straw, and in front, the wide, white reach of the Hawkduns and Mt Ida at the end of the road.

Cleaning up

For the first time in weeks the land has dried out enough for me to ride my bike from the house to the road. The sky is grey though, and rain clouds are coming up from the south. Bartali and I settle into a good pace up the valley. We talk about the river, the Manuherekia. The community has big decisions ahead – setting the minimum flow, balancing the farmers' needs for water against the healthy life of the river. Yesterday we spoke at a meeting in Alexandra. Ahead of us lie submissions, careful readings of data. Somehow, as a community, we have to negotiate a way through conflicting needs.

At the top of the valley we turn left up Lockharts Hill. The wind helps from behind, and with my new control over the lowest gear I go up the hill without too much struggle. Even so, a gap begins to open up again.

'Does it matter if I get a bit behind?' I call out.

'No,' Bartali calls back.

Good.

'Unless it means you're not trying.'

Shit. I push down harder on the pedals.

The sheep in the paddock next to us are newly shorn. Some look up from grazing as we pass by.

'I didn't know shearing had started,' I say.

'It's been going for weeks.'

'I haven't seen any sheep driven up the road.'

'No, but I've seen the vans with shearers going through the village,' Bartali says.

Ahead of us a dramatic sky lets enough light through to shine on Mt St Bathans. It's a big mountain and one I don't get to see from my own place – the willows growing along the Ida Burn are too profuse. But here it is, rising ahead of us, the sun shining silvery in places on the slopes. The slick patches of tarseal on the road shine silver as well.

Will I be fit enough to cycle to the St Bathans turnoff? I ponder this, turning the pedals, keeping up with Bartali. And then the question is over-ruled by a flock of sheep bobbing in a mob across the bridge, cars banked up in front of them. More sheep for the shearers.

'We're not going to cycle through those,' Bartali says, and in a flick I've turned my bike around, heading back towards the Ida Valley.

It's five kilometres from the Ida corner to the village. Downhill, with a head wind. I tuck in behind Bartali's wheels. We cruise into the village at 39kmh. And there outside the public toilets is a van. Oops. I remember I'm on toilet-cleaning duties this week and had almost let the day slip by. While Bartali does intervals, skimming back and forth through the village, I carry mop and bucket from the General Store to the toilet, clicking along the footpath in my cycling shoes, helmet on my head.

Spring

There's something in the air that has us looking around, thinking maybe the cold is almost over.

'It must be spring,' I call across the road to Ken. He's with his ute and dog outside the General Store.

'Yes, I was watching the birds flutter around the digger in my front paddock this morning. They were looking to nest. And I knew then it was spring.'

Yet on the bike the air is chill. My feet are so cold they're numb.

'Look at that big-bugger cumulus nimbus over Mt St Bathans way,' Bartali says.

We ride towards Wedderburn. There are sheep clustered on a far ridge, but nothing's going on at Becker's woolshed yet.

As well as shearing, the farmers in the district are scanning ewes, Ken told me.

'If they know a ewe is having twins they'll put her on good feed. If there's a single they'll put her on tougher pasture so the lamb doesn't get too big and cause problems at lambing.'

'Are you there?' Bartali calls.

'Yes,' I call back. Up the 'gnarly little bastards'.

'Just set your own rhythm going up the hill. Pedal in circles,' Bartali says.

On the last hill I stand up on my pedals to keep up with him, recover on the final sweep to the corner.

'What a lovely downhill ride,' I say, and then realise it's because I'm in his shelter. I take a turn at the front into the head wind.

The third time I pass him he calls out 'Relax your forearms!' I realise my hands are clamped with determination to the handlebars. We sprint to the village. I tuck in and go with him, hands low on the bars, but he burns me off as we pass the General Store.

Home to a spirulina smoothie, a shower and some time by the fire before the evening shift at the hospital.

A wee ride

This morning, frost, and yet, beyond the silver sheen of grass and tussocks, a line of eight cyclists. The first group of riders on the rail trail for this coming season. Later in the day, the cyclists safely at their destination, the wind comes up strongly from the northwest. The long grasses on the side of the road bend over from the force of it. Later still, the wind slightly dropped, Bartali texts – *A wee ride?*

Mostly I'm not the one to text that. Mostly my motivation is at the lower end of the scale. And yet, it's a gift when someone else encourages you to exercise. As often as I can I say yes, even if I don't feel like it. Who does feel like biking uphill into a head wind? My rule to myself, while I'm so unfit, is to respond positively. And not to moan on the ride or ask when we are going back, but to suck everything up and keep pedalling circles.

We turn a few times on the road – up the valley or down the valley to ride? – and settle on Lockharts Hill, uphill into that head wind. Sheep either side of the road, a lot of low cloud skudding along, the sun deep behind a cloud and, in a burst of sunshine, the new gravel over the repaired road section glinting like splintered glass. Perhaps schist flakes, Bartali thinks.

On this ride either I'm fitter or Bartali is riding more slowly, but I manage to keep up with him all the way to the top. 'Good riding,' he tells me as we cruise over the hump. We go past the bridge where the sheep had mobbed last ride, and past the old stone house on the corner of Hills Creek Road. The wind is relentless. Being under-dressed for the cold doesn't help either, though I do have newspaper down my chest.

The sun glows on the slopes of the Home Hills and the Hawkduns below the snow line. I think of lines from Brian's poem 'Place': 'the light is like honey/ on the stems of tussock grass, and the shadows/ are mauve birthmarks/ spreading/ from the hills'. I watch the hills as I ride.

The 'wee ride' is an hour. A good workout. I can feel the strength returning to my body. We're not going long distances or high speeds, but there is a difference, a determination perhaps, returning. And to test it, I pull out past Bartali on the home straight into the village, pumping my legs, watching the number on the speed board turn over to 36kmh. In the west the clouds begin to glow, long forms of pink and gold.

Fields of lucerne

It's not blossom, but without my glasses the small withered crab apples adorning the trees through the village look like red flowers, as if the trees have bloomed all winter. It's a fine still day and we head up the valley. Neither Bartali nor I have newspapers up our shirts. That's how we know things are changing around here. And the snow level is edging up Mt Ida: more brown flanks now than cap of white.

The biggest change is the green. A paddock stretches away to the west, a fur of bright green. Baby lucerne. Around here a crop of lucerne lasts thirty cuts, or twelve to fifteen years, Barry Becker told me. A long-term crop that does well in this dry valley.

We turn left towards Mt St Bathans, still shining with snow at the head of the valley. I struggle to keep up with Bartali. Days away have taken the edge off that frisson of fitness I'd gained. But at least I'm out on the bike, and I'm grateful to Bartali who, nine times out of ten, will be the one to say 'You keen for a ride?', and who makes me work, challenges me. No slacking going uphill into a head wind with him.

'When there's a yellow line, listen out for cars coming up behind you,' Bartali says.

There's a plume of dust on a side road ahead of us as a fertiliser truck accelerates uphill. Dust! The first we've seen all winter.

'It must be spring,' says Bartali.

Sheep lift their heads as we pedal past, and some call out baaing, and we baa right back at them. They're closely shorn, and big bellied.

'They'll be lambing soon,' I call out.

'I thought they were wethers.'

'They don't have a button on their waistcoats,' I call back. (It's a term I learnt from Ken.) Though I don't have glasses on, and nor can I see udders. With the discipline of the yellow line, Bartali's back wheel and the rough edge of the road, it's not the time to crane my neck to study the sheep.

We climb up St Bathans hill ('Good riding,' says Bartali) and over. He tells me to take the front. And here's the best part of riding for me. Out in the front, speeding downhill, the rush of the wind, a big curve ahead and no other traffic on the road.

On the sprint home Bartali hits 38kmh into the village. I laugh again, standing on my pedals and trying to keep up with him. I make it to 33kmh. But it was a good ride, the longest I've ridden since starting training again.

We bike home towards the mountains, the Hawkduns and Mt Ida shining white and the road leading straight ahead, between the fields of lucerne.

Merino

Sleet moves in a swathe across my paddock towards the Dunstans. Bartali and I sit by my fire discussing the possibility of a bike ride in an hour when we've both done some work. I'm reading Gaston Bachelard's *The Poetics of Space* (five years after building my strawbale house) for research for an essay. So much to take in, and before I can put my book down, there's Bartali outside in his cycling gear.

We're both dressed warmly, the sheets of newspaper up our chests a trick Bartali learnt in 1954. His father was training his cousin, Alan Larkins, who went on to become a New Zealand champion cyclist. They wore woollen bike shorts then, Bartali told me, with chamois leather sewn in across the seat.

We head out in our layers of merino and lycra. The snow has melted from its overnight falling on Rough Ridge and Blackstone Hill. Surprisingly, as the cloud lifts to show the hem of the mountains, not too much has layered up there. A localised Ida Valley snowfall then.

The sign saying the road is out has gone so we turn up Hills Creek Road. But the approach to the bridge is still out, the tarseal rumpled and buckled by water. Bartali lowers the bikes to me.

There's been some upset in the valley about the state of the roads here and the fact the village had flooded at all due to the build-up of gravel upstream. A newsletter sent to each of us advertises a meeting about the roads with the mayor and council staff. 'Please come along with an open mind and civil discussion,' it reads.

There are paddocks of young lucerne along here too, but the low grey cloud tarnishes everything with a dullness. On Rough Ridge a shaft of light illuminates a stand of poplars.

The sheep up Hills Creek still have their bulky wrinkly coats, though early yesterday morning on the way to work I noticed Barry's woolshed was lit up, sheep mobbed under the bright lights and a wool truck, fully laden with bales, parked next to the shed.

Under a gum tree three bulls rest as we bike past. They're chewing their cud, biding their time until mating season.

Wind

Hail for a change, this spring morning. A friend rings and I leave the fire when the sky quietens and go outside to weed the lavender and bulbs while I talk to her. We discuss the coming protest about the big irrigation schemes in Canterbury. And now that the sun is flickering to come out, we decide that rather than talking about our concerns, the best thing we can do is go for a bike ride (though we're 150 kilometres apart).

Bartali and I head up the valley. The low hills and the Hawkduns are in shade, but Mt Ida stands shining, an unearthly sight on a dull day, the 'wind fierce out of the west'.

We strike the full force of the wind going up Lockharts Hill.

'Are you there?' Bartali checks on me. *Baaaaaaa*, fifty or so sheep call back.

'Yes,' I call too, and dig in to keep up with him.

In summer the sheep are tawny brown in tawny brown fields. Today, the day after shearing, they're like a Rinso ad – bright white sheep on green grass.

Out on the coast near Dunedin there are lambs cavorting in the paddocks, willows sheened with green and old plum trees beside the road frothed with white. But here winter has barely lifted. No lambs yet – they'll be late September at least. The willows and the poplars bare. Only the lucerne and the grass know its spring.

'Another nice little pinch,' Bartali says, as we go up the second hill.

'Does it have a name? I call it St Bathans Hill,' I say.

'I call it Hills Creek Rise,' Bartali says. 'It's really the saddle between the two valleys, the Ida and the Manuherekia.'

Whatever it's called, the wind is strong. On the way back I stop to take a photo of bales of lucerne, plenty of feed left yet for stock. A gust of wind nearly blows me off my bike.

Coming home down the valley, there's a cross wind.

'This is where riders will drop people in a race,' Bartali says. 'If you can't handle a cross wind you're out the back. And riders won't put up with people sheltering if they're not going to take a turn. Otherwise they could come out at the end with a sprint and win the race.'

I shelter most of the way up the valley, tucked into Bartali's left side. The sprint is on at the end. I give it everything. Sparrows burst out of the tall yarrow, bouncing and lifting ahead of us, like blimps in the wind. Thirty-nine to 37kmh. Bartali wins.

Water

How long has it been since I've ridden my bike? Months. So much building work, travelling, teaching, deadlines. But now with the sun out after the flood and the whole valley tingling with energy – the sheep being shifted on Rough Ridge, the lucerne being baled up Ida Valley, the flooded Ida Burn still clattering and thunkering across the paddock – what better way to start again than to go out among all this?

'Are you there?' Bartali asks, before we even pass the end of my paddock. The long round trip ahead seems longer. I push down on my pedals to keep up.

'You know, I've lost a terrible amount of fitness,' I tell him.

'A lot of that is in the mind,' he replies. So there'll be no excuses today.

We turn up Hills Creek Road where the 'road closed' sign is up again. Ahead of us water flows across the road. I thought it would be shallow enough, but it's surprisingly deep and swift, and over my pedals. The road surface beneath the water has been stripped so that it is like riding on a jagged riverbed. My bike wobbles and stays upright, though my feet are soaked and the water splashes as high as my chest.

'That was worse than I thought,' I call out to Bartali, who is already opening up a lead again.

'Of course,' he calls back. 'Are you still in proximity?'

'Yes.' I push hard again, in time to catch up before the next flooded patch. I'm glad we didn't head out yesterday, although it would have been spectacular. We'd tried to cross my paddock to see the flooded stream up close, but couldn't make it across the new swift streams that had sprung out of nowhere.

It has been such a wet spring; in some paddocks the grass looks waist high. In one paddock, four massive black bulls share the grass with sheep and lambs. There is enough for every creature. Green, green as far as the eye can see.

'Like somewhere in Southland,' a friend said yesterday, 'not Central.'

Along the roadsides the wildflowers are blooming – white oxeye daisies, yellow potentilla and buttercups, and the yellow of broom and gorse. The remnants of matagouri have a faint white flush of delicate blooms. The air smells of damp grass and lucerne drying out, of the pea-scented broom flowers and the boggy mineral smell of water deep in drains and paddock hollows.

We ride back along the rail trail. Bartali thinks this is because I don't want to ride over Margot's Hill, which could be true, but I tell him I want to see the flooded streams close-up. It's the best ride I've had up the valley on the rail trail – warm sun, no wind, and the exhilaration of riding through farmland to the burble of water. I feel like I'm smiling inside.

We stop on the rail bridge over the Ida Burn to watch the flood. 'Disaster tourism,' Teri Gardyne said at Hayes Café yesterday. Because who doesn't like to watch the power of nature, when you are safely above it?

Summer

We are cycling through summer. In the paddocks the foggy grass and cocksfoot are tasselled and downy as wheat. Bartali and I head up Hills Creek Road, over the bridge the farmers patched up while waiting for the council. The evidence of flood still lies in the tangled branches in the fence lines, though below us the Ida Burn is torpid, slow, only a few pools and a thin stream running between them.

A farmer is discing a bare paddock. The air smells of warm earth, and though rain is forecast to come at last, today the soil and the dry grass on the flats and hills is testament to long days of heat and no water.

As we bike, a flock of dark birds swoops and turns above the road in front of us. Starlings, perhaps, or blackbirds. We haven't once been harassed by magpies this season.

Further on paddocks are mown for lucerne, some with the long yellow trails of dry lucerne ready for baling, while clean-shaven paddocks have rows of tawny bales. The haysheds are beginning to fill. And there's a smell in the air of jam cooking. Philippa, who used to run the Ida Valley Kitchen Café, lives near here, and I imagine, as I sniff, that she has a deep pan of raspberries boiling.

'Stay in top gear,' Bartali says, 'and we'll go like the clappers.' We do. The wind fresh as we hurtle down Woolshed Road. There's the smell again of burnt sugar, though no houses in sight, a warm, sweet waft of air. Perhaps it's the fields of lucerne in purple flower perfuming the air, or the patches of broom, their seedpods ripe in the heat.

Riding on country roads like this it's easy to imagine we are part of this land and rural life, just two other creatures moving through it, like the herd of cattle who fling their heads up at the sight of us. They're fawn and black and chestnut. They break into a gallop like wild horses and charge along the paddock beside us, their coats glossy in the sun.

I hear another noise behind me.

'Car!' I yell to Bartali.

'What? Another one!' he calls back. It's the second one to pass us in an hour.

But soon, back on the tarseal, all illusion of oneness dissipated, we're minding the traffic now, and the trucks, and the wide road distances us from the animals and the golden grass. And then again, like a blessing, that smell of jam as we ride into the village, the rural air still holding sway.

Autumn inspiration

Rain and sun, rain and sun ad infinitum – a recipe for autumn and mushrooms. When I left the valley two weeks ago it was golden with drought, and now I'm back to a greenness so rich the lambs are belly deep in lucerne and my potato patch is rejuvenated and flush with white flowers.

Bartali and I, both rusty, head out on our mountain bikes for the easy route up Hills Creek Road. We'll go around McKnight Road, race the long hill down to the main road, over the hill and home. The easy route, a thirty-eight to forty-five-minute circuit with lots of downhill. My go-to route when I've lost fitness and want to regain my confidence. There's a slight head wind, grey clouds, and both of us are riding bare legged, though not for much longer with this slight chill in the air.

On McKnight Road, only two black swans on the lake in all its ruffled expanse. A farmer next to it tilling a paddock. And with the green and the moist air, if there was any doubt it was autumn, there are mushrooms – circles of fat white and brown shapes scattered over the paddocks as far as I can see. I've been eating mushrooms every night since I got home.

There's no traffic on the road or any other people about, just the sheep as we pass by: the weaned lambs fat and woolly, and in another paddock the smooth-coated mothers, strong shouldered with rounded bellies. The rich grass an unexpected bounty. Most farmers are hoping to get a third cut of lucerne. Last night the contractors worked nearby till almost midnight to get a crop in for silage.

My bike won't go into top gear, so we stop at the top of the incline and Bartali lifts the chain over for me. Then we're off, speeding towards the woolshed and beyond. I even pass Bartali, bent low over my handlebars.

One car overtakes us on the highway, then a truck, Central Stones, going the other way with a load of schist towards Queenstown. Then two laden fertiliser trucks. We swing into the village. I feel stronger in the legs than I imagined I'd be (top gear, even over Margot's Hill). It's the type of ride that inspires me to keep going, to keep getting back on the bike and experiencing this valley with nothing but the sky above. Aahh, fitness, thank you, you haven't deserted me yet.

Sun in a country valley

It hasn't been a year for wildflowers, despite the earlier promise. The blue viper's bugloss straggled on through summer, but it's the white yarrow that now dominates the verges as we cycle past. At a distance their massed plantings are frothy and bright. Up close the flowers are delicate and airy. And on each side of the road the long driveways are lined with yellow – yellow birches, yellow poplars, golden-yellow oaks and my favourite, the yellow-green-turning-scarlet rowan trees.

We'd waited a morning for the forecast rain to come and be over, but by lunchtime the sky was still low, the clouds dense and foggy about Blackstone Hill and the ground sogged. We hadn't seen the sun for days. When Bartali and I take our road bikes out, it seems so long since I've been on my bike that I almost fall on the road trying to edge my foot into the pedal. We circle, testing the wind, and head down the valley. Winter almost upon us. I want to see what's happening in our valley.

The Ida Burn, for a start, thrumbles and rolls in muddy waves under the first bridge. We rattle over the repaired sections of the road. Easy to see where the flood damage has come from. The stream each side is almost up to the level of the road. The paddocks mostly green and close cropped until we come upon one golden as if it is mown tussock. In the weak light I can't tell what crop it is, but turning back see the crunched-off dry stalks of lucerne, a paddock grazed not mown. In some fields the heavy-coated sheep are grey with moisture; other fields are empty, the sheep already on the tops or near the sheds waiting to be crutched.

Yesterday in the rain I'd asked a farmer, 'Are you pleased about the weather?' And he'd said, 'No, I've got 12,000 sheep to crutch and it won't stop raining.'

'It's not easy crutching sheep in the rain?'

'No, it's a bugger of a job.'

Robert, who'd finished crutching his sheep a few weeks back, was having trouble getting the rams up the hill track to the mobs of ewes.

'The road's so greasy at the moment,' he told me, 'we can only just get them up the hill two at a time using four-wheelers with tractor-grip tyres.'

'Couldn't they walk up?'

'No. We're taking different breeds of rams to different mobs of ewes in particular blocks. And because the blocks are 600 to 900 metres above sea level and the land has steep gullies, we take the time to drop the rams off at different locations. The ewes then have ready access to them. Rain is so needed,' he said, 'but sometimes it makes the job at hand a lot more difficult.'

Above Bartali and me the sky is still laden with clouds. We keep a good pace down the sodden valley to the eleven-kilometre mark where it begins to rise in a long stretch of hill.

'We'll turn around here,' Bartali says, and for the first time ever, faced with a hill I say, 'I'm fine to go up the hill.' I *want* to go up the hill. Normally I'll be thinking *please turn around, please turn around.* Maybe it's the plant-based diet. Extra power. Or else because there's no wind-driven hail, no snow, no icy swathes of wind or uphill stretches. We turn around though, and Bartali, pointing back behind his wheel, says 'tuck in there', and we're off. Eighty-five percent effort, kilometre after kilometre. My lungs feel good. I remember times we've done this and I've fought to keep each pedal pushing, watching the back wheel and the fenceposts, just hanging in. Today we whizz along the tarseal, up and over Margot's Hill, though I still can't catch Bartali, hill-avoider or not, the gap opening up between us every time I let my focus drop. Then a scramble to get back in behind.

'Are you there?' he'll ask, 'Yes.' 'Are you there?' 'Yes.'

At the end of the valley the cloud is lifting. There are the Home Hills, tawny and rugged with gullies, and a strange light in a line along Blackstone Hill, brightening to lime a lucerne field, flaming the willows. Sun, how missed and how blessed on a country road.

Winter again

Heading down the valley into a snow-threatening wind, Bartali and I realise we've been softened by our warm fires and have come out unprepared – no warm head covering or jacket or double gloves for me, and Bartali has fingerless gloves on. Our faces are chilled by ice and our fingers numb. The Perendale ewes, newly crutched and with heavy fleeces, are thick in the low paddocks. There are rams with them, black-faced, portly built, and presently sitting in the grass. The birds are numerous too. A flock of sparrows rises out of the dock and yarrow on the roadside to land and sit on the fence wires, round and textured as walnuts. Further on in a wet green paddock, twenty paradise ducks flap up as we ride by.

We take a turn left onto a gravel road, one we haven't taken for a year or more, a road that rises up and up in a series of roller-coaster hills. The road surface is a fine clay.

'I remember when most of the roads in Otago were like this,' Bartali says. 'It's a shame they're not still, no one travelled too fast on them, and each side the tussocks stretched away.' We look about at the green fields stretching to Rough Ridge and up its flanks. Not much tussock left in the Ida now. Further down, though not where we're riding, the valley opens out and the golden tussock lands have given way to irrigators and the black shapes of cows as far as the eye can see. Up this end Rough Ridge is close, the skyline dotted with tors and rock features. Here it is sheep country, as it has been for over a hundred years.

Bartali rides the rougher centre of the road, letting me take the smooth track and in his lee, protected from the wind.

'You're a gentleman,' I say.

'There's always a place for courtesy and kindness,' he says. His fitness and greater experience on the bike means that in winds he'll take as much of the brunt as he can. There's no traffic on the road and we swoop up each hill, standing on our pedals, and down the other side. At Anderson Lane we turn and bike back onto the highway. Trucks now, and four-wheel drive utes. It's the Brass Monkey Rally in a few weeks, when over a thousand motorcyclists come to camp in the valley, warmed by log fires.

'Let's go look at the bonfire,' Bartali says, and we bike up into the dam paddock where the tents and motorbikes will be. Built of whole trees and logs, the main bonfire pile stretches above us. Further along, stacks of firewood cut for the campfires. There's a sound of machinery in nearby trees, and as we cross back over the bridge, the Ida Burn high and wide with water, I begin to worry that the crashing and snapping of tree trunks that we can hear is too close to the old huts in the paddock, small wooden and corrugated-iron huts used for farm workers in the early days of farming here. A row of three, big enough for a bed each, tucked under the willows.

And there is the digger, reaching out and snapping branches above the small huts, one with its roof already stoved in, another with a crumpled wall. I take a photo and can't bear to watch any longer. Three little huts beside a stream, part of our unappreciated history.

Hoar frost

It's possibly the coldest day in the valley and Bartali and I are of one accord. We need to cycle through the hoar frost. Otherwise how will we know how it feels? Actually, that might be my reason, but Bartali wants to keep training, frost or no frost. We head up the valley where the iced willows line the Ida Burn, and for once broom is a beautiful sight. The frozen yarrow stalks look like ice sculptures along the verges. Apart from the occasional burst of colour in the landscape, like the lime-green plastic-covered rolls of lucerne baleage across the paddocks or a yellow road sign, everywhere is monochrome grey, black or white.

I wondered how it would feel cycling in this weather. To breathe, I find out, is like sniffing chilled vodka straight up my nose. It hurts. I cheat by breathing through my mouth, which is covered in Bartali's red merino balaclava. He didn't wear one – he said he managed okay when out training the other day. But today is harder. His fingers, in one pair of gloves, are 'screaming' he says. At least he has newspaper down his chest. I wear a homespun jersey instead, as an experiment. The chilled wind enters even this. But I have two pairs of gloves.

We're riding to the top of Blackstone Rise. Up Lockharts Hill the breathing is easier. The fences are no longer latticed ice. The grass is tawny gold. The pines are green.

'Perhaps this hill was above the inversion layer,' Bartali says. Behind us the fog is unfolding along the Ida Valley.

The old Blackstone Hill school, to our left, was once hidden in a forest of trees. Now it's safe from falling limbs, a small, abandoned building on a wide hill. It's the only structure left of a goldmining township with fifty businesses. On the way home, back into Ida Valley and the white breath of fog, we meet our neighbour Peter in his truck with chainsaw. He calls out that we're mad. Not long after we get home he will arrive at Bartali's with a load of fresh-sawn pine.

In the meantime, we still have to get home. My gears won't change but we decide it's too cold to stop and fiddle with them. We head home into the wind, past a farmer's frozen pond and the stream that runs into it still and white as well. Past sheep nonchalantly grazing in the iced grass, past our friends' houses with their beautiful iced fruit trees and birches, and home, where a magnificent white crab apple tree arches over the stone wall.

Late winter, Ida Valley

Months, again, again, since I've been on the bike. But maybe today. Today is fine, still, a late winter's afternoon with the light pale on the hills. I said to Bartali when we were in the car, 'I'd like to bike to the cemetery, I think I could do that.' The minute I open the car door and stand in the cold fresh air, I retract. I've just got over the flu. It's too cold, too far. I can't do it, I say.

I weed instead, kneeling on the damp lawn in my dress and tights to pull rye grass from around the climbing rose and lavenders. At least I am doing some activity outside. Bartali walks around the corner of the house.

'What about we ride up the road to the corner and back, just that. You could do that,' he says.

'Ok. But I'm biking in my dress.' Then it's not too big a deal.

I find my helmet and gloves and sunglasses, put a cycling jacket on over my dress and wheel my bike out to the road.

'We could take Hills Creek Road and stay off the main road,' I say, and that way we bike over the bridge and can see the Ida Burn running high after days of rain. Not flooded though.

We bike uphill along the gravel road, the paddocks each side of us blanched of colour, the grass frost-wilted and tawny. Not tawny like the summer drought, which is more golden, but as if the gold is poured over with grey.

There don't seem to be any animals as far as the eye can see, all the way to the Idaburn Hills at the foot of the Hawkduns. Around a bend the smell of turnips in the air, and then there's a field of young black steers. They run back from us then turn and stare, their faces all pointed one way, and the air smelling like soup. Beyond them a paddock of sheep, merinos, heavy and grey with their wool.

'They could be last year's lambs,' I say.

'Or are they hoggets?' Bartali wonders.

'Two-tooths?' I realise how little I know. But they are not the breeding ewes further up the valley, shorn and white and thick-bellied. These have the leap of the young about them still.

My legs feel fine. We bike to the corner of the foothills road and keep going. Now that we've come this far, I want to bike all the way to the cemetery. I remember the last time I came this way; I was on my own and it was snowing. I'd biked in the flattened track of a car tyre. The streams in the paddock were frozen. Now, the gravel road is damp, the flinty stones pressed down into the soft surface, the ditches running with water.

The gate is shut at the cemetery, the lawns newly mowed, and it looks like the graves have been sprayed, so empty are they of rampant growth and flowers. It was summer when we weeded here, and hollyhocks towered over headstones.

My friend Polly's grave is a receptacle for all that her visitors bring: figurines, clay roses, a pebbled heart with a pencil sticking out like a mast. Hawthorn berries scattered scarlet on the dirt. I walk over to the hawthorn hedge and pluck purple-red berries and bring them back to sprinkle. I stand there for a while with her.

It's 4pm, and the air is chilling when we get back on our bikes. It's just the hills and the mountains covered lightly in snow, the wide fields of grass opening away from us. A late-winter palette of grey and white and fawn.

I remember now that when I'm not biking the presence of place recedes. I sink back into gazer again. I know the light on the hills, but I don't know the sweet smell of the lucerne fields or the sound of the Ida Burn in roar under the bridge. I'm not waiting to see lambs born or the wildflowers bloom. On the bike I know the lift of the road, the power of the wind. I know the crescendo of lungs, heart, breath. It is our bodies that move us through our days, that let us experience topography and our place in it.

'What's productive here/ is what's in your heart,' Brian writes in his poem 'Van Morrison in Central Otago',

> sworn through your eyes,
> ears, the flitter of the
> wind in your hair;
>
> The smell, the taste
> of air from the mountains,
> off flats where the river
> runs from somewhere north
> to somewhere south and the sky's
> forever.

At the corner of Nelson Road a silage pit is open. For metres afterwards the air smells of rich fruitiness, and then we are onto the home straight, Ida Valley Road, downhill. An exhilaration of speed, of joy in the workings of the body; legs pumping, heart thudding, dress flying.

In the Midst of My True Life

IN THE MORNING the sun rises over Mt Ida and shines into the bedroom of my strawbale house. If it's winter there could be snow, ten centimetres of white over the stone wall, or frost silvering the grass and toetoe. In summer there'll be wild poppies ablaze with red, the grass as tawny as the hills. And if there's a wind, the rippling tussocks will show which way it blows.

> … Wind again. The clouds
> fused over Blackstone Hill. Maybe snow
> the paper says. The tussock flicks like hair …

In that time after our ending, I drew the design of a house where I could wake to the sun and write. There'd be a blaze of gold in my room. Now, the mud walls hold the luminescence of lime. The floor is pressed and trowelled earth, oiled with linseed. It glows with its own richness – that of beginnings, of standing right where you are. Yellow curtains at the window.

Outside there are sheep on Rough Ridge, making their way through tussock and tor.

I once read of a writer who lived in her bedroom. She did everything there – eating, writing, reading. But she didn't have a house to finish. Another coat of earth plaster for the sitting-room, another coat of lime.

Women write to me and say: *I always wanted to build a strawbale house, or a rammed earth house … and now my husband has died … now my partner has left … now I'm on my own I want to …*

We have forgotten we can build our own houses, how capable we are. I am anchored in this house where every wall holds the memory of my hand.

Perhaps more people would like to build a natural house but curtail themselves. I held a dream of building a natural house through thirty-seven years of marriage and partnership. What is it that prevents us from realising our dreams? Is the force of conventionality too strong? Perhaps when you lose much of what you value, you're ready to take a risk and do what you believe in.

> ... I'm juggling fear and awe:
> my private regrets, a past snuffed,
> the fact of this house at all ...

Perhaps, when we have suffered loss, the drive to build a life that holds more meaning can lead us to consider building our own shelter. Like Carl Jung who, filled with grief at the death of his mother, built his stone tower at Bollingen. 'At Bollingen,' he wrote, 'I am in the midst of my true life. I am most deeply myself.' As I helped build my house, with each beam I lifted into place, each nail, each bale of straw tucked into the wall, each handful of mud and hawk of plaster – I, too, felt that here, along with a structure that arose physically in the landscape, I was remaking my life. Giving myself strong foundations, a protective roof. Not only a place to dream, but I, the dreamer, created anew in this place, with the hills on each side and the mountains at the end of the road.

What if one person says to another, *We could build a natural house* – and does just that?

Following conscience rather than convention. 'Such an act is no mere vagary,' American author, farmer and conservationist Wendell Berry writes. 'It is the basis and essence of political liberty.'

> ... be a warrior in terms of what it takes.
> It's not just the cold,
> sometimes it's the strength to get up.
> To rise up. Restraint
> is another word for imagination ...

I want to trust that we will one day rediscover natural building. Could this help provide more sustainable housing solutions? Auckland architect Min Hall asked exactly this in her master's thesis, and concluded: 'Straw, timber and earth ... have the necessary material characteristics to produce enduring, healthy houses on a sustainable basis.'

But why hasn't natural building become mainstream? Hall quotes Ellen Jackson's 2009 master's thesis 'Self Reliance and Earth Building in New Zealand': 'The largest reason why the surveyed population did not want to live in earth buildings was because it was unfamiliar or unknown to them.'

Staff at Placemakers are hardly going to start talking about mud. ITM doesn't advertise house-lots of strawbales. I want to shout from my high-pitched roof, 'Mud rules! Lime is the queen of all building materials! Build from this earth, and respect it!'

In this I know I am going against convention. At the pub one night when the locals heard I wanted to make an earth floor over my concrete floor, the ribbing began. Especially from the trio at the bar – farmer Barry, truck driver Grim and tradesman Wayne.

'You'll be able to plant potatoes on your kitchen floor,' Barry said, and laughed.

'And after that a crop of beans!' said Grim. He laughed too. I just smiled back at them. I felt on solid ground. The ground that comes from being free to believe in something and having the strength to carry it out.

'How deep are you going to make it?' asked Wayne, at least beginning to think logically about it.

'Half an inch,' I said. He nodded, but still looked bewildered. 'On top of concrete?'

On top of perfectly good concrete. I had no funds to cover the concrete with anything else. I had piles of leftover clay and sand in the back yard and a part-bale of straw. I'd learnt how to handle a trowel. It seemed immensely logical to me: if you have the chance to make something yourself, out of something as free and natural as dirt, then do it.

'I have a question for you, Barry,' I said.

'Ask away.'

'Why are the bulls roaring? I heard them out on the hill when I was finished on the mixer.'

'I've got two in one paddock, and three in another,' Barry said. 'And I'm thinking now there's probably five in one paddock. And being males, they've got a bit of sorting out to do.' The three males laughed.

The publican brought us free chips. Enough for everyone in the bar. We stood around the counter with our cold beers, hot fries.

'Give us a yell and I'll come over and have a look at what you're up to,' said Wayne.

'Making her kitchen muddy,' said Grim, the truck driver who would come even on a Saturday if I needed sand, driving the company's JCB up the road with a scoopful. And Barry, turning up in the middle of foot-trimming, blood on his cheek, to bring me baling twine for retying the strawbales. They might not understand the work I do, but they respect work, and the doing of it.

That night in bed I went over the day: the straw sifted through an old wirewove bed, the clay too. And wedged under the bowl of the concrete mixer, the old bath, finally full of a lumpy, grainy mix – a recipe I hoped I'd got right.

Would it work, though? I'd never seen an earth floor being plastered, or even seen an earth floor except in a book. I held that picture in my mind – the glowing floor. A floor made out of what was there.

Once a year the local high school brings the high-achiever class here. We meet at the pub for coke and chips and a talk. Sometimes I bring them to my house. I help them make lime wash. I show them my walls. I want them to feel how simple it is to contribute to your own shelter. I want them to have hope.

If someone calls in when I'm plastering, I pass them a bucket of earth plaster. 'Put your hand in it,' I say. 'Put some on the wall.' There's a joyous response. The mix of fermented straw, clay, sand, sawdust and water is cool and tactile in your hand. It squidges between your fingers, it smooths and curves under your palm. You are a child crouched by a stream again, enthralled with mud.

When I massaged earth into the contoured shape of the walls, I thought the house could be a living, breathing animal. The house could be its own entity. And why not? Each time I come home I greet my house like a companion. Does saying 'I love my house' and 'My house lives' sound mad? Time after time, when people first step in the door, there is a silence akin to awe. 'It feels different,' they say. They breathe, and look around. They're not sure what it is, other than the hush of the walls. I stand beside them, feeling it too.

How vulnerable we were during construction. My son-in-law Sam and I, up on the top beams with the wind against our thighs. Forty-three degrees and only the outline of walls for shade.

up with the drill, the hammer,
the Skilsaw,
sun like lava
on my thighs and knees …

When building a house, you're aware of all a house gives you. From
the first roll of building paper and run of iron screwed to the joists, shelter
begins. With the first wall blocked in comes respite from the wind. And
when windows replace tarps, light returns and with it the line of hills and
the grass.

Where I sit in my house looking out to the hills, I can imagine my
home from the foundations upwards. Those first few days on site, the pick
falling into the clean dark earth, and each scoop of the spade tidying the
foundation trench so that it ran true and deep behind me. 'In our wake,
the path we have taken trails out behind us,' Kathleen Dean Moore writes
in *Wild Comfort*. In her essay she is on a small boat, lost in mist and waves.
In the same way, my future was uncharted before me, but the wake of the
straight-sided trench – that showed I was going somewhere. I even had
plans.

And I know the pitch of the roof: on top of the ladder holding on to
a red sheet of iron as it bucked in the northwester, and Sam calling 'Hold
tight!'

I know the quarry my lime came from, in the dry hills at Dunback.
Calcium carbonate, friend to humans for 5000 years. Burnt at 1000°C it
becomes calcium oxide. Added to water, calcium hydroxide. Mixed with
sand (one part lime to four parts sand) and water, spread over the earth
plaster, it fixes carbon from the air and returns to its natural state, calcium
carbonate. An almost carbon-neutral substance to use in building.

… When I get up I start the mixer
tumbling, add lime, the sand
flecked with gold.
I know what joy is, spreading this
simple cloak on mud …

Beautiful, ethical, breathable lime.

When I spread the earth plaster onto my concrete floor, that joy returned. I lifted cold handfuls out of the bucket and pressed it onto the concrete. Five, six, seven handfuls. Then I took my wooden float and smeared them, pressing, the mud shifting under the wood until it became one smooth surface. I changed to the steel trowel and pressed it firmly on the surface, running the trowel in one gliding motion until the mud became a sheen of flat floor. And when that area was done, I turned to my bucket for the next handful. Hour after hour. The floor my earthen wake behind me.

There are strengths we can lose when we are two, by becoming dependent. By forgetting what we are capable of. While we were building together, Sam pulled me up when I didn't rely on myself. 'You can't go on in life always expecting a man or someone else to do things for you,' he'd say. 'You have to work out ways to do things yourself.' This to a person who couldn't get lids off jars. How much strength does it take? Do what I can, I learnt, then do what the job requires. Plastering under the curve above the window, the trowel upside down and the mud falling again and again into my face and onto the wide windowsill, until one small amount stuck, and another amount stuck, and some fell down and some stuck. Cursing inside at my ineptitude. The mix too soft, but trowelling it up anyway, over and over, until the job was done.

How hard it is to do something when you lack the skill. To want my work to be excellent and know that it isn't. To know I'm doing the work that skilled women have done for centuries – only not in my culture.

How hard it is knowing my own dad was a fine plasterer who taught my brothers but not me – because I didn't ask, because I wasn't interested, because I didn't know about earth, or that he would die, or how plastering is not just solid or fibrous or gib-stopping but with earth can be the foundation of shelter. It's an art. And it's a simple, joyous pleasure. Self-taught, I inch towards that sense of pleasure in a job well done. My father running his hand over someone else's work, and then that nod of respect to craft.

Just before it went down behind the willows and the bulls began to roar, the sun flung its last colours up onto the mountains so that the white snow became gold and tangerine. When I turned the mixer off, there was the sound of the stream again, rippling under the willows on my boundary, a clattery noise under violet clouds. Water, and sky, and the feel of the mud mix cool in my hand, it's solidness akin to what I felt inside, a linking to the natural world and to all the women who had gone before me, the *enjarradoras*, the earth plasterers, the ones who made shelter for their families.

Here the sheep are big bellied on the lower slopes, and newly shorn. The black bulls pace the fence line. I tuck a tarpaulin over my mud, weight it with boulders. The tawny brown mix gives me hope for a future where I can still provide for myself, still dream of things that are possible, resourceful, and respectful to our planet. Still strive to do more than I think I can.

When the day is finally done I move my laptop to the small table near the fire. The orange glow warms the stone surround, keeping the house a steady heat for me and for my drying floor. There's a wind up, blustering and buffeting the west wall and singing in the flue. The house has its arms around me.

Barefoot Running

Every Saturday we piled in the car to go somewhere to win a race. It was our thing. Sullivan girls. The other kids used to groan when we showed up in our bare feet.

I thought we were awesome because we were all such fast runners and our secret reason was barefoot running, but the secret reason behind that was probably that we hardly had any shoes ha ha.

I remember trying to repair shoes and mend socks at night. Shoes were an annual thing so you really had to get it right. I remember bare feet a lot, I even won the cross country in bare feet in high school though it was partly on the road.

1995: LAST NIGHT my daughter and I went for a run along the causeway. The sun was down; the tide was pooling and going out, enough light in the sky to be reflected. Hana and I walking along then stretching against a lamp-post. 'People will think we're trying to push it over,' she says. Then she starts running in front of me, moving effortlessly away, her long thick pony-tail swinging from side to side. Once, on my birthday, I biked beside her while she ran. A seagull flew out of the sky and landed on my handlebars, and sat there as I biked down the road watching my daughter and the twilight sky.

I grew up in a routine of Sunday School and Sunday roasts, white shoes and socks for church, our mother playing the hymns. Life may have remained like this for me, as it did for the tall, straight-skirted aunts with their hair crimped in waves and their hands so nimble in the kitchen on a Sunday, raspberry tarts with custard and apple pies. But our father fell in love with his young badminton partner and we became, in 1967, the only family we knew whose father didn't live with them. Instead, after our mother shifted us out, he lived in our home with another woman and her children, who slept in our bedrooms and climbed our trees, though they didn't inhabit my cupboard above the wardrobe. I used to climb up there and cram in with my cousin and sister. We'd write lists on the wall: people we liked best or worst, animals we loved, plans for our futures and, from me, lists of all the novels I'd write. Below us, Mum played loud classical music while Dad was out, dreaming her own poignant dreams (forbidden to play the piano while her housework wasn't done) and probably pleased we wanted to sit in a cupboard for hours instead of requiring any attention. Until the day our father stopped the car ten houses down the street from home and picked up another woman and her two children, packing them in with the four of us kids, to go on holiday with us instead of our mother. From that moment, our life as we knew it was over.

On visits to see Dad in the weekends we had to be quiet, be second best, keep our opinions and our memories to ourselves. We couldn't mention our mother. We had to be good. We weren't good, but we didn't know much better. I once rang my step-mother. I was ten. 'This is the police,' I said. 'You're under arrest for adultery.' She hung up. What was adultery? I didn't know. I'd heard the word from relatives. It had a menacing, authentic tone for what was happening to us.

Our mother, a teacher, took us (two girls, two boys) to live in a country schoolhouse, despite one local woman's petition to stop a solo mother teaching the district's children. My mother was thirty-four. Though scientists say the result of one chance event does not affect the result of later chance events, I was thirty-four when I took my children (two girls, two boys) to live in a country schoolhouse.

I asked my mum, now eighty-five, what was the best and worst of being a solo mother.

'I can tell you straight away the best,' she said. 'It was the freedom. My word was law. I could decide what to do.'

'Like how you took us to the Russian Ballet?'

'Yes, and played for all the musicals, you girls at every rehearsal. The thing that gives me the most heartache? Not having time. Saying to you, I can't, I'm too busy. That's one of my biggest regrets.'

I ask my children how it was for them. I have to remind my middle daughter to reply. Merrin, who is bringing up her three with shared custody, says, 'I've been so busy, but I'll prioritise.'

Their answers:

It sux when your childhood is shattered, when the comfort of having your mum and dad around all the time can't be true anymore ... but step-parents ... even worse ... I envied families with parents together yet was also drawn to them. At the same time, I told myself the story (or perhaps you told me) that going through this would make us stronger, that we could face anything.

When Mum and Dad split up, I remember everyone at church making a big deal about it and hugging us like we were expected to be upset and crying. But because Mum and Dad told us clearly and honestly the reasons then I just accepted it. I don't recall ever longing for my parents to get back together. I knew they both loved us and that was all that mattered.

There always seemed to be so many of us all around, there was so much noise and chaos there didn't seem an obvious family role missing. Maybe there would have just been less noise and chaos if we were a nuclear family. I remember my brother Nick looking after me heaps – my person to look up to. Would have that been different in a two-parent family? Probably not. I think I was so much more focused on siblings than the count of parents in one household at any one time. And sometimes they weren't all there, but I was in the mountains with all the animals and trees and occasional birds with broken wings that I could try and rescue instead.

It was quite lonely and boring in the day as all the other siblings were at school and I was at home on my own on the orchard while Dad was at work (but still around). I remember seeing Mum in the supermarket but I wasn't allowed to talk to her. I was too young to be doing one week off and on between parents.

When we went to Dad's, and he was working late, it was just unspoken that we kids would learn how to cook and make dinner.

I learnt how to make dinners out of nothing by scanning the pantry and fridge and making something weird and healthy.

My mother writing songs. My exercise books of stories. Such dangerous notions of independence and creativity which did, in the end, go on to blow up our lives, one way or another. If you have a vision of yourself that is clear to you (as each child knows in the pit of their stomach), it behoves you to remember that knowledge – that is, who you are – and stay true to that.

That does not mean leaving your wife for your badminton partner, or your husband for a man who loves mountains. With the hindsight of grief and the knowledge of rupture, I would say: cleave to your knowledge of yourself before you choose.

Oh, but that idea – that 'hope and grace' might reveal themselves in my life again.

How I changed, from anonymity – at school, at the bank, at community events, from being so merged with the status quo that I didn't know this was only one stream I belonged to when I followed all the rules – to conspicuous outsider, a sudden inexplicable shift in how society viewed me; from the unlabelled Mrs Sullivan to solo mother, as if overnight I had become a different person. Lining up at Social Welfare for a slip to buy my daughter a calculator because the teacher has threatened her with detention if she turns up one more day without one. Lining up in the stationery store with my form and being told not to choose the expensive version. Going home and crying – but with a calculator. Repeat this even for a bra for my daughter. Like being married to a conglomerate of people who can bring you in anytime and question you. Ah, yes, the investigation unit of Income Support: Mrs Sullivan, we have allegations. We have a letter from 'anonymous sources', from 'decent citizens' … And yet to feel so grateful at the same time. In Moscow I've seen a small baby wrapped in grey cloths on an icy footpath while the mother begged. I know the safety net of a benefit.

'Your children will never amount to anything' – Mother of my daughter's friend

'Mum, why does the radio have to say things like kids from solo families don't turn out well? They shouldn't say things where kids can hear that.'

They have become, variously: scientist, engineer, analyst, teacher, finance manager, builder, national sport champions, animal rights activists, entrepreneurs, managers, business owners, environmentalists. Parents.

Living in a broken home environment made me want to get out of there asap. I knew university was the way people got out of town. Education was key. You brought us up to know we could achieve anything.

Having no money growing up was definitely a motivation to get a proper job and earn money for the lifestyle I imagined. I learnt that a passion (writing) is not a good source of income and you should definitely have a plan B.

I didn't really know all the amazing careers you could have and thought it was just simple things like doctor lawyer teacher builder etc. I'm now on my sixth career (engineering). I have such a drive to do things that need to be done without needing to wait for the perfect moment first, i.e. travel, study, marriage, kids, renovating, shifting. Decisions are hard but outcomes are always manageable once you stick with a decision. It will work out.

Leaving too soon and staying too long – that seems to sum up my marriage/partnerships. Five children. Various configurations of family: shared custody, single parenting, step-parenting, daughter to me, son to father, step-parenting again, single parenting again. On and off the benefit.

Once it felt like Income Support forced me back into a relationship:

'You can go back, or never have anything to do with him again, or you can look at a six-month jail term for benefit fraud.'

'But he's the father of our two-year-old and she loves him. And it's not good how he treats my teenage daughters.'

'You tell your daughters to buckle down and do what he says.'

No, you, Income Support, get fucked.

Except I did go back.

I remember I couldn't wait to leave home and get away from him. I was probably a bit of a bitch to Mum because I couldn't understand why she stayed with him. Her reasoning didn't make sense. She didn't want to be a single mother. But we were all fine? It briefly made me think being a single mother was something bad.

'Woman may not be as abject as she appears,' says American philosophy professor and feminist Debra Bergoffen. 'She too may be buying time. She too may be protecting another value.'

Yeah. Trying to make this thing called love and family work.

When I finally achieved my dream of leaving home and getting away from everything that upset me, it made me realise how much I loved you all and how family is important, no matter what form it is in.

What I wanted then? A decent car. Snacks. New clothes. New knickers and matching socks. Something other than brown bread sandwiches and apples for school lunches. Above anything, I wanted Mum to be ok.

One of the earliest and most widely spread stories in the world is that of the Swan Maiden, the heavenly bird-creature that is captured by a mortal man who steals her wings and buries them. She is forced to remain earth-bound and has children to him. A myth, I think, that speaks to the action of grief allowing the return to the sacred.

No longer did she glimmer in the moonlight. Her husband came home nightly and beat her, and in the day she cried. She hid her tears from her children. Each tear splashed down on the earth and wore away the floor. Her tears washed down, down by the main post of the house, and there one morning in the mud was a feather. She lifted out her wings.

'Come!' she called her boys. Agile and clever, they stood nearly to her head.

'I must go now. When you are older, you will find me.' And quickly, while she could, she put on her wings and flew up to the sky, her feathers shining ...

The older kids were working part-time after school and weekends, at the supermarket, in the apple orchard, the packing shed. One day I applied for and got a job at Talley's fish factory. I went home and told my oldest son, Rory.

'No, Mum. No,' he said. 'You're *not* going to the fish factory.'

I looked up university courses instead. If I took masterclasses with writers Kate de Goldi and Dinah Hawken at Victoria University, I could be paid the same on a student allowance as at the fish factory. So, I went to university. Uni was in Wellington, in the North Island, and we lived in Motueka, in the South Island. I used my visa card to fly, one day a week, to the city. When my card maxed out after a term, I switched to extra-mural study through Massey University. That's how I achieved a master's degree.

('Don't put anything highfalutin' like that on your application form,' WINZ again. 'You're only going to end up a cleaner.')

Mum, I'll put some thought into this soon. But I don't think you need to emphasise the poor stories too much ... Single parenting doesn't have to be parallel to poverty.

I agree. In terms of 'single parent poverty hardship' it was only really that six months or so that we lived in a tent that resonates. Going 'camping' on a school trip where we slept inside cabins, but getting ready for the trip out of a flooded tent and all my packed gear was wet. Other than that – I don't think about us being a 'solo parent family' that much either.

My last year at home it was just my sister Evie, Mum and me. I felt like I had a lot of freedom to do whatever I wanted. I had no constraints on what was masculine. I could develop my spiritual side in a single mother situation. It had a big impact on my life. Maybe if I was in a more masculine environment, I wouldn't have picked up on all the things that mean a lot to me now – meditation, yoga, healing. If sport is a societal measure of masculinity, the fact I was top of my sports (rugby, athletics) gave me confidence to express that feminine side. I definitely had the freedom to be who I wanted to be.

American essayist Akiko Busch: 'Diminished status can, in fact, sustain and inform – rather than limit – our lives … can, paradoxically, help us recognise our place in the larger scheme of things.'

I want to give my kids the secure 'nuclear family' upbringing that I didn't have. I got lucky with Sam, but also there is something in 'always turning toward each other', being a team, being assertive, working together, asking for what you need. As for childhood, we got through it. We learnt what we could handle and what we didn't want to repeat in our own lives. We learnt to strive for happiness and find our own way in life, not be stuck in a rut or put up with bullshit. We learnt that not everyone in the world is nice (avoid those types) and not everything works out the way you want (but keep looking forward and choose your own path). That's all, the kids are up.

As a single mum now, my upbringing has made me want to open my home to kids going through tough times at home. Lots of girls from single mother homes stay with us from time to time to have a break. They say their mums are crazy and too strict. The mums say their daughters are out of control. I try and channel my calm, earth mother and be a yes mum.

What I value? Making things fairer. Being a good listener. Being a good Dad. A safe home without conflict and enough money to easily get by and provide for my family. My view with kids now is that you must teach them all the things in the world that won't be fun for them if someone else is teaching them/telling them off.

'I showed those country families who didn't want me in the district,' my mother said. 'I taught their children to sing.'

Going by my own experience, my middle daughter said, *I don't think you really get to know yourself if you are partnered up from a young age and have kids early. My girls and I go over the timeline of their future lives – a lot different to mine:*

University or similar after high school.

Not married until at least 25. Or not at all.

No kids until at least 30. Or none at all.

Don't rely on your partner for money.

Always have a career to fall back on.

Travel.

Visit Mum often.

The Snow of 63

We drank, Mary, at the diggings, I swear
the whole camp wet the baby's head.
I know full well, you did your best.
I've sent gold with Tom to Chamonix

and on to you. We made sixty ounces each
the last six days, and though the snow keeps falling,
I still have oats and pork and tea
and the gold under the snow still calling.

With Tom gone, Stan and I have shifted claims.
We've pitched our tent near Drunken Woman's Creek.
We heard the gold was better here, the gains
worth frosted ground, in weather bleak.

Does Paul thrive? And are you treated kind?
Up here, we have to look to one another.
Snow still falls, and food is short,
I gave the last of my oats to a young mother.

And Tom's not back yet, nor packers come.
They say the track has succumbed
to immensity of drifts and wind, and lack of shelter.
All I have is flour and water. Yet I dig on, my hands so numb.

Mary, I have grave news. Stan is dead.
He slipped and froze on the path last night while I slept.
Now torment and anguish fill my head
and even if I did have bread

I couldn't eat when there are young ones here
chilled and gaunt-faced, and their father dead
too in the blizzard, it's feared. And all our flour gone,
and nothing to spare.

It's a howling world, and a fight against sleet
and the wind, and the snow piled deep on our tents.
The ground too hard for a pick, no sense
in gold now, or wealth, or pretence when it's food we crave.

Oh, for the sweet smell of milk and sun-rough hay
not these endless knives of white.
This letter a last missal, too cold to write
relentless the ice, the wind, and the night.

Once we ate speargrass root, now that too has gone,
and the men who went over the tops haven't returned
nor those down through the treacherous gully.
Tomorrow it's my turn,

and I'll take my turn, the others too weak to leave.
Thirteen men, three women, two children, no food or reprieve.
Is Paul warm? Are you fed? That's all I wish now
for you, and for all of us here. My dear.

Dear Mrs Miller,
With this letter from Robert John Miller, one hundred ounces of gold.
Both found on his body, the 1st of September, the last survivor
to come down from the Glacier, on the Old Man Range.
He died of the frostbite on the outskirts of Chamonix
and is buried in Dunstan.
May peace be with you.
Sergeant Fraser Brown.

Love, Loss and the Fraser Basin

> There's gold, the jolly fellow promised,
> the Alpine Reef on Old Man Range,
> most encouraging descriptions, two shifts,
> a hut and victuals, and in summer
> balmy nights beside the stream …

WE LEAVE for the top of the Old Man Range, behind Alexandra, on a fine summer's morning. Four of us want to explore the old quartz mine workings in the Fraser Basin: contractor John Breen, former commander of the NZSAS Graye Shattky, former Poet Laureate Brian Turner, and me – grandmother, natural builder, writer. All of us bound by our love of and advocacy for the high country, for the open spaces and the purity of water over snowgrass and rock.

John's truck graunches over the deeply rutted track into the Kopuwai range. Rock tors loom over us, as rugged as sculptures. Tussocks gleam in the sunshine. Towards the crest the groundcover gives way to fellfields of daisies, the white mountain celmisia, and then a tundra of grey-brown hummock fields I haven't experienced before. Freeze–thaw cycles have created small waves of soil that are covered in the spongy grey cushion plant raoulia, and green mosses. Cloud drops over us. The view from the truck window becomes unearthly: only the mist, and the rippled formations of slumpy earth.

Last night it snowed up here, though it's mid-summer. We pass pockets of white and in one place, in the shelter of rocks, snow lies deep across the track. We plough through the drift, the truck holding and skidding briefly then churning its way back onto the gravel.

'Hopefully we'll get sun again today and it'll melt that snow,' John says.

We descend into the basin, the hummock fields behind us, the tussocks silvery in the mist. Far ahead on another slope is historic Nicholsons Hut, a small corrugated-iron shed poised above the creaming rapids of the Fraser

River. We climb out of the truck into air that is sharp and cold and foggy. Graye pours us a hot coffee from his thermos and passes around thick sandwiches. We crouch in the cold mist, coated and hatted, gloves in our pockets.

I don't know where John plans to take us. I only know he wants to show us the sites of his latest book, *Nicholson's Folly*, the story of the great Alpine Reef gold stamper. The stamper was hauled component by component up to these heights in 1882 for Charles Nicholson, with as much hope and ingenuity as men could muster.

The bullock wagons that came this way had spent days rolling through the schist-covered Otago country. They crossed the Clutha River by ferry at Beaumont and passed through the towns of Ettrick and Roxburgh, as clanking and stupendous as a circus, teams of six, seven or eight pairs of oxen. The bullockies walking beside them knew each ox's name and character. They cajoled them uphill, one wagon after another along the tor-lined ridge. Perhaps the men crouched here, where we are, and lit a fire to boil sugared black tea, the oxen with their heads down against the wind, the mens' calico tents no barrier to snow and chill.

> First, we have to build it –
> the hut, the shed, the battery,
> the water wheel and revetment,
> our jobs dependent on the gold.
> But will you pay us, jolly fellow,
> will you pay us what we're owed?
>
> Three months in mist and thumping
> wind, to the galloping pulse of iron.
> Three months, no shine
> while the promises flowed, and the bullocks towed
> and the south brought snow
> though it's summer …

'Even a brief glimpse of what we were is valuable to help understand what we are,' says Irish writer Dervla Murphy. I think of how Nicholson asserted his power over nature: the creeks dammed, the trees in the next valley cut down for fuel, the lives of packies and miners risked in these extremes.

We leave the truck on the side of the track, pull on backpacks and head into the tussocks under a sky now warm with sun. There are no discarded wagon wheels, no iron left behind, nothing to lighten the load of the wagon-train that came this way. At this stage of the journey the oxen pulled sleds to traverse the bogs and tussock, each one bearing two tonnes or so of machinery, including the components of the water wheel and the crushing battery. The mountain ridges are like encircling arms and the far tors like sentinels, guarding the way. Over this moraine of buried boulders and gravels left behind by an ancient glacier, the oxen heaved.

Nothing left to mark their trail through the basin, but there, John points to show us, a raised, spade-formed earthen exit from the narrow Fraser River. We splash through, the water clear and cold over the tops of our boots. Here the men dug a ramp for the oxen and their sleds. The great loads clinking, harness rasping, the grunting of beasts and their breath billowing in the air. They strained with their legs thick as a man's forearm, up over the top to the tussocked plateau, the men shouting, their tension over.

Tussock gives way to bog and stream. There, John points: peatbogs where the men cut fuel, sharp spadefuls of peat which they loaded onto sleds and carted off to dry until dusty and rich with the forgotten humus of plants. Peat warmed the men and fuelled the cooking fire. One hundred and forty years later, the rectangular marks of the harvest still show.

Each springy footfall of ours lands on a cushion of moss where flowers garland the bog with their frail simplicity. After a trail through the high and smoky tussock, it's as if we have come upon heaven. All of life before this moment and the next – a life of time constraints and traffic and chores, of loss, of disappointments and frustration in one's own endeavours – has given way to the peace of a wide and quiet place, where each living part fits into the whole, each making the best of its rightful habitation. Even the black-backed gulls that lift off the small tarn ahead of us and wheel about in the blue sky, calling out that lonely seaside cry, have found a place here to breed and grow, as have gentians, blue tussocks, slim snow tussocks, and the *Gaultheria nubicola* (cloud dweller), its thick green leaves tinged with scarlet and white bell-shaped flowers that look like currants. Each plant thriving in its place, like instruments playing their part in the wide sweeping music of Sibelius' *Finlandia*.

Above us a small brown bird hovers on an updraft.

'Skylark, I'd say,' says John. 'They'll hover and sing to you, whereas a pipit will scurry.'

And through this landscape, as if dreamed, a rivulet of water, a stream perhaps a palm-width wide, burbling and swishing, and where it falls a few centimetres over stones, a frothing and cascading. The smallest of rivers, and yet it is a river – the beginning of a river – and will join the other freshets gurgling across this basin to become the Fraser. Illustrious water.

We stoop to fill our water bottles. Graye tips out his town water to replace it. Brian has brought an empty bottle, knowing the mountains and the water. I've carried two bottles filled from the spring on Rough Ridge at home, but when Graye offers me a drink from his bottle, I accept. The water tastes of peat and moss and rock.

'You could write a poem, Turner,' says John. 'About all this water.'

I think of Brian's lines, 'This land's part of what's called nature … I say our place is hallowed ground./ I say we should care for it more.'

We have brought our hearts and minds and breath to this basin. Why come at all, following an ancient invisible trail towards the remains of the Alpine Reef stamper, imagining men who worked up here, beyond the ridge from which could be seen the tents of civilisation, beyond help when the snow blew frigid and deadly in their faces, beyond hearth and home? Why remember them at all, and the craving in their hearts for gold; and why stand now beside the fallen blocks of stone, outline of the one shelter provided for them? Why imagine the hut standing, the mutton simmering, the wet boots steaming by the fire, the laughter of the men released from wind and toil – if not to be aware of the turns and grinding nature of fate, 'embracing and comprehending the great cyclic renewals of creation', as Roman Emperor Marcus Aurelius wrote? Comprehending it. Why, if not to be aware of our own demise, and therefore the need to listen to the mountain stream music, to be reminded of all that's sacred and right in nature and in our own beings as well? To 'care for it more'.

> The likelihood is we won't.
> For all that, here's hoping,
> here's to a decent attempt
> for all the right reasons.

> –*Brian Turner*

'We shrink from change, yet is there anything that can come into being without it?' Marcus Aurelius again. I chose his book from a shelf in my daughter's house after I'd flown to her, bags crammed with plastering tools and no room for my own books.

Perhaps what I really want to talk about is loss. Is history loss? Can the actions of people be raised up, as if we stand on shoulders, upon shoulders? Or are we doomed to repeat, repeat? The belief we have against the insistence of reality: the hail, the snow, the ice, the distance. The implacability of nature.

Once, on another mountain slope, my partner and I lay in the bracken on our own land, facing to the mountains of Kahurangi National Park, while our daughter chased wild goats. It had snowed the day before, but on that morning it was hot, the bracken crackly and all the white gone. Our daughter's voice ricocheted around the slopes. Her father said, 'I've been thinking about us.'

The possibility of us was so fragile. Yet how do you let go of hope?

Once, we lived on a mountain. We carried timber out of the forest on our shoulders and built a hut with our own hands. It was our first attempt at building. When the wind raged the mats lifted from the rough planked floor. Snow blew through gaps in the wall between the window frame and the corrugated iron. We cooked stew all day on the fire and in blizzards went out to check on our horses. My foal Rosie was born up there, above the snowline, the rocks and fallen logs familiar under her hooves.

When Rosie was young and untrained, her mother gone, I went out one day into the mist to search for her. I climbed onto the great slab of Lookout Rock. Through gaps in the cloud I could see the town far below. Was my future down there, or up here? Either choice would lead to grief. If it were just the three of us … but it wasn't. I had older children who were my life too, and they needed to live in town. By my own actions, my life was as divided as the mountaintop from the sea.

There was a scrabble of hoof on rock and there was Rosie, my mountain horse. She stepped across the stone slab to stand beside me. I didn't lift my hand to her shivery neck. She was still wild, her own being. But she stood as I did, looking out towards the ocean and the town, the mist like rain on her chestnut coat.

In the Fraser Basin, the others look briefly at the rocks of the fallen hut and move on through the tussock towards the quartz site. I stand there, almost unable to walk away. I think of a poem by my friend Grant Clauser: 'Every kind of passing/ leaves a field of grey remains,/ boulders stuck in place, settling through/ years into their own memories.'

Sides of mutton had been kept in a snowbank behind the hut. Inside, the cook (who left unpaid, John wrote, and sued for the sum of £23 in lost wages) rolled dough for damper and banked the fire. At the other end of the hut, palliasses stuffed with snowgrass were suspended on sacks strung on a wooden frame. The workers drank whiskey at night while wind and snow howled outside. Today, sun, the snowgrass supple and shining in the breeze. I lay my hand on the rock stacked in the remnant of wall, this outline of shelter a poignancy 'that stands on shoulders of sterner/ deeper woes, and speaks for them/ in ways I can't say why'.

I turn my head and watch the three men pushing uphill through the tussock.

One thing nature has that workers do not have, nor women and children, nor subjugated races, nor religious or gendered minorities, is that in the end nature holds all the power. Even if it takes a rise of more than two degrees to show us this. But here in the Fraser Basin nature certainly batted last: not enough water to run the water wheel and stamper, the small streams icing over, the weather too harsh (up to thirty miners had earlier died of exposure in these mountains), and the distance too great over the steep rocky pass and through the boggy swamps to bring in regular supplies of food and fuel. The rocks would not yield. The ice and wind and snow were such that men could not work the necessary shifts. By 1883 the Alpine Reef was abandoned.

> Over Bendigo way the miners went on strike
> they were turfed out of their houses
> and the manager's wage went up ten shillings
> it went up ten shillings for the fracas

of cutting men's pay. Eight shillings a day
we were promised we'd be paid, ten hours
and a half day on Sunday
and the jolly fellow with his rum
calling out for songs and fun

but I'll not sing for him when
the lantern's dim and the howl
of sleet and hail in the wind
when the ice descends and your only friends
are the blazing fire, and the money ...

In the Fraser Basin, a grasshopper sits on a piece of quartz beside a filled-in tunnel where men once wielded picks, the rock walls clanging with the sound and the fog and chill air above, where rivulets of stream began to freeze. The men's hands warm only where palms met wooden handles.

The rocks would not yield.

Perhaps there was never enough gold here, despite the assertion in the *Tuapeka Times* that it was 'one of the main or leading reefs in this island', of gold 'freely seen with the naked eye'. Or perhaps, as John thinks, there is still gold up here, trapped in the glacial moraine; gold ground out of the mountain and reburied by the rocks themselves.

We sit for lunch, contemplating the climb up shingle and rock to the ridge above us, all the basin we'd walked across stretching below. We lean our backs to the cliff and eat our sandwiches. Fields of turf and rocks, and the music of a rivulet running through moss in front of us.

To the left beyond the ridgeline, beyond Teviot Valley, beyond the Knobby Range, the Lammermoors rise. They, too, woven with tussock and rock, as wild and silent as Kopuwai, in part because of the years in which Graye and Brian wrote, pleaded, submitted, raised funds, spoke at court hearings, stood up for what was wild. To our right along the humped tops of the Old Man Range and beyond are the valleys where the Nevis begins. That river flows undammed, knowing only its own path of rocks and cliff, tumbling pure as snowmelt to its confluence with the Kawarau, again in part because of Brian and Graye and the environmental society, their months of research and reports, submissions and court hearings. And these hills and this basin have for years been the place where John has brought his own and many other teenagers on school and overnight trips, teaching them how to make snow caves, spending nights with them under the cold stars, skiing, swishing over these boulders and memories when it's snow time and all about is transcendent with white.

'Take me back to the – blue hills?' sings Brian.

'The *black* hills,' says Graye, and they both sing, 'the black hills of Dakota, to the beautiful Indian country that I love'.

'It could be the blue hills,' Graye says, and quotes to us from the SAS ode, taken from lines by James Elroy Flecker:

> … we shall go
> Always a little further; it may be
> Beyond that last blue mountain barred with snow

Later, I look up the words from Flecker's 'The Golden Road to Samarkand':

> We are the Pilgrims, master; we shall go
> Always a little further; it may be
> Beyond that last blue mountain barred with snow
> Across that angry or that glimmering sea,
>
> White on a throne or guarded in a cave
> There lies a prophet who can understand
> Why men were born: but surely we are brave,
> Who take the Golden Road to Samarkand.

In our mountain forest the air was lime green with moss and lichen and leaf, the fantails swooping after midges, the bellbirds calling, their song more liquid than the stream. In summer the hut was sun-dazed, our horses nodding under the beech trees, the air buzzy with flies. In winter, snow came like a blessing. We didn't have crops or stock, only the remnants of logs the early settlers had strewn across the steep face of our forty hectares. In a blizzard snow flung sideways into our faces, our lips and cheeks stinging. We kept the fire going twenty-four hours a day. In daylight I pulled a sack across the slope to find the smallest broken pieces of beech for kindling. Our fire voracious, wood our only currency for heat.

... Coming out of the bush unexpectedly
and there it is, or in moonlight,
on your last legs,
coming up through snow,
a candle on the table, and outside
possums skulking ...

Until the time came, I used to wonder how would I bear to walk away from the hut down the side of the mountain and look back for the last time: the peaked roof, the chimney free of snow, and behind it kawakawa, tōtara, beech (red, silver, black, hard).

From the ridge we scrabble down a sheep track. When it becomes steeper still, Graye and I sit and slither down the slope over the tussocks, their shining strands an easier transport than balancing on the shingle.

On the way to the remnants of the stamping battery I film a stream pouring over a drop.

'That's a burbling stream,' says Brian, stopping, like me, to admire its clarity. 'We meander like a stream,' he muses, 'or rush down a cataract, or sometimes we're swept over a fall.'

This stream is the one that led to the great water wheel, the wheel that was hauled by oxen, piece by piece, up to this height, and 100 years later was hauled down again by men and machinery and erected outside the Alexandra museum and art gallery. I wish it had been left here, and the hut too, the kettle beside the empty fireplace, to show us how things were. But in those 'great cyclic renewals of creation', as Aurelius wrote, what went up came down. The land returns to what it was. The tussock grows over the timbers, fallen where the stamper once stood. The stone walls of the water races shift, crack, fall or blend back to earth. The peat bogs are protected now. There's silence. And protection, too, in that to be here we had to walk hour after hour through the basin, watching each footstep, carrying our own victuals. Before dark and snow return, we'll be gone.

But will you pay us, jolly fellow
will you pay us when it snows
will you pay us from your credit
we know how far that goes,

will you pay us when you're shirking
and your dream's no longer working
but it's us out there cutting peat in the bog
hauling rocks and digging ditches
in the sleet and the fog
and our dreams, our own dreams of home
and company and repleteness
gone soon we'll be gone

'Salvation,' Aurelius wrote, is

to see each thing for what it is – its
nature and its purpose.
To do only what is right, say only what is true,
without holding back.
What else could it be but to live life fully – to
pay out goodness like the rings of a chain, without the
slightest gap.

Perhaps the workers – the miners, the manager, the packy, the cook, the race-man, the bullocky, the blacksmith – perhaps they knew the nature and purpose of their tools, their animals, the sphere of their knowledge. But the instigators of the project – Nicholson, his partner John Kitching and the investors – disregarded the reality of the project: the elevation, the wind, the isolation and chill of the Old Man Range.

Not only did Nicholson attempt to dominate nature, he also dominated his workers upon whom the project depended. In the end they may never have been paid. Instead, they became pawns in his drive for accumulating wealth. Before the Alpine Reef project Nicholson had been bankrupt; post-reef, he leased a hotel and went bankrupt again. John's book records that Kitching, the owner of Beaumont Bridge, had charged an 'excessive and ruinous toll' on oxen and horses until the government intervened and bought the bridge. Kitching, whose shearers' contracts were 'incredibly tyrannous', also had a history of not paying wages, holding off until forced to pay by the courts, as did some other early runholders. Many labouring men were unable to stay the distance of a court case and simply walked away. The houses of miners who struck for better conditions at Bendigo were torn down. In the cities too, in the sweatshop conditions of textile and clothing factories, women were paid little for their labour.

What I'm looking at here is a history of subjugation. I begin to see that the foundations of our culture and society were laid within a framework that saw wealth as taking precedence over the rights of others, land included. The 'back-bone of our society' was built on this. In *The Forgotten Worker: The rural wage earner in nineteenth-century New Zealand*, John E. Martin writes that most rural workers were itinerant and low paid, their shelters bare-floored shacks with tiers of bunks under leaky roofs.

Gold-miners gum diggers bushmen grubbers navvies shearers labourers coal-miners threshers ploughmen …

'Perhaps of all men to be found in the colonies, the strongest, bravest, and hardiest is the … gold-miner.'

–Edward Tregear, first secretary for the Department of Labour

Instead of walking back beside the peat bogs and the small tumbling streams, John leads us higher onto the flank of the mountain to follow the old water race. At each step I marvel at the construction, how men with spades dug level and true, negotiating the slopes and the boulders. The raceman and his horse would have come this way regularly, checking the flow, removing impediments. Now the race is broken in places, the ground beside it undermined by water. Graye and I both fall into unexpected holes hidden by grass. Yet the sun lays gold on the tussock as far as we can see. Below us the Fraser River grows stronger. No longer a freshet, it surges over rocks.

I remember riding Rosie, her ears pricked, chestnut legs swishing through mountain grass, our food and water packed in saddlebags and our daughter ahead of us on her small brown pony. The sing of water far below us then, too, the Brooklyn Stream on its way to the Motueka, the air cool and clear. And at sunset, not silent hawks but the kea, the mountain parrot with its scarlet wing feathers and plaintive cry.

To give up all that has gone before – time, and the brief incandescent moments of sparkle on tin, of sun on river and comradeship around a fire. The pain one has been through, as if this much pain must be equalled by that much gold. Or to stay, mind shut to all other pathways that must open up the moment you turn your back on this one. Was there an incremental tipping between pain and the decision to leave? Did it take disaster to tip the balance – such as the mine manager at Alpine Reef who broke his arm and never went back? Or would a person wake one morning in a frosted tent, hands crimped, boots frozen, knowing the rocks will hold what is theirs to hold, and decide: now it's time for home?

> A glacier paused and emptied
> its pockets, lightening the load.
> Could this be what it comes to?
> The dry debris abandoned
> when one era ends
> and another begins

> *–Grant Clauser*

At my daughter's house the lime plastering is done, the walls trowelled smooth and my tools packed. Her father is here too. It is the first time our visits have coincided. For two years we have both helped on the house, he with building and wiring, I with lime plastering and gardening, separately and as invisible to each other as the elves to the shoemaker. Now we stand in our daughter's garden and wave as she leaves for work. What can be said about the tumultuousness of love with its needs and wants and expectations, filling the loneliness for each other and standing up for each other, all the things being with someone gives you: the self-interest side of love. And what can be said about the aftermath that ends like this, in peacefulness beside rampant tomatoes and white petunias: a flowering of grace, a feeling so free of grief and longing that it seems as clean as cold air.

When he smiles at me I remember that young man I loved fiercely, and that's all I remember for now. We have redeemed ourselves to ourselves. He is still boiling barley and carrying hay for Rosie in her old age, still making wine and jam from the plum tree that blushes wild with white in springtime. I'm still writing poems, essays, stories and submissions, and tending to my grandchildren.

This could be a happy ending: to stand in the truth of your own life and see the other person in the truth of theirs, and recognise that. Be happy for that. Sometimes we don't manage this together. Sometimes we have to do this on our own. Sometimes we have to stand beside the rocks of a wall that has fallen into grass, that is merging back into earth, and know that this is how it is. And the wind clean and sharp over your cheeks, and the sound of the freshet of water, the smallest, clearest spring, on its way past your feet to become river.

The Art and Adventure of Subsistence

1.

I came from a neighbourhood where the violence was as underground as the potatoes in the vegetable gardens behind our houses. We didn't speak of it to our friends. We didn't display it in public. But what do I know about how it was for others? I like how Joy Cowley writes in her memoir, *Navigation*, of the weary policeman who would arrive on his bike when her parents were fighting. I like how she looks back with compassion, rather than shame.

When my own mother called the police on my father, the cop car pulled up in our drive and neighbours clustered on the footpath.

'I should have hit her years ago,' my father told the policeman, who seemed to concur with him, my mother told me later. It was the 1960s.

I wonder how much frustration boiled over into violence, then: my father rubbed narrow into a life he didn't want, pulled out of school and made to work in his father's plaster factory; my mother forbidden to play the piano when what she wanted was to write songs. And secretly did, winning Studio One, a national song-writing competition, under a fake man's name. She didn't think a judge would let a woman win.

How does this need, and drive, for meaningful work affect us? I think of that childhood cacophony of despair and mis-matchedness, the underground rivers of desire and the 'weary policeman'.

In a quest to understand the deep needs of people, Chilean economist Manfred Max-Neef and his colleagues at the Center for Alternative Development in Santiago developed a detailed set of nine authentic human needs, which he proposed are common to all, regardless of nationality, education or social or financial status. Emma Kidd, in her book *First Steps to Seeing*, discusses Max-Neef's work and lists these needs:

Subsistence Protection Affection
Understanding Participation Creation
Idleness Identity Freedom

'[I]t is not just an inability to meet our need for subsistence that leads to poverty,' Max-Neef's team asserted, 'but that if any need is left unmet, "poverty" is created.'

2.

When I teach writing on a week-long course, I allow a day for the study of nature – a slow, sense-filled study, some of it in silence, to give students an opportunity to change the way in which they look at the world. I first began sending students into the garden ten years ago. They were to isolate their senses and spend time really seeing, smelling, touching, listening. They ran their hands over bark, leaves, ferns; inhaled tree trunk, thistle flower, grass blade; listened to birdsong and wind (and traffic) and watched light shine on the ripple of green.

Emma Kidd studied the art of seeing with scientist Henri Bortoft (a co-worker at one time with Max-Neef). Bortoft, a British lecturer and writer on the philosophy of science, was a scholar of the work of eighteenth-century philosopher and scientist Johann Wolfgang von Goethe. From the study of Bortoft and Goethe's work, I deepened the way classes spent time with nature. Students studied a plant in a process Goethe called 'exact sense perception', until the wonder of design and uniqueness revealed itself. Goethe believed if we look respectfully and clearly at the phenomena around us – that is, at all that makes up our living, natural world – then we have the chance to understand that we are but one part of an interconnected society. This way of perceiving would lead to social transformation, he hoped, and would possibly protect our natural world and humankind from extinction.

3.

In a small garden at Rosemont College, where I teach in summer, you walk down stone steps past a stone statue of a child angel under a maple tree to a grassy opening and planted borders, where wild raspberries thrive along with milkweed, comfrey and ivy among the hostas, coprosmas and ferns.

How easily the world gives new life; how plants, given sun and soil, will fill a place with their exuberance: the low-growing, spreading plant with its leaves splayed in rosettes, the ivy clambering over the top, the comfrey's coarse leaves softly bending, and the thistle, that wild imposter with its tufted purple flowers, surging through them. The thistle's perfume adds to that of the wild raspberry. Their sweetness is for the bees, their minerals for the soil. In that garden plants find a way to live abundantly together and to contribute. How vulnerable we are if we do not have even the basics of connection.

The oak's trunk is so old and cracked that an ivy weaves through its apertures. I press my nose to an insect hole in the worn bark, my skin against the tree's rough skin, while birds cheep and chime. And there it is, a smell as far off as the days when I polished my mother's oak dresser with a cloth: the sweet oil fragrance of tree.

4.

My mother told me it is always good to have two strings to your bow.

'I'm a teacher,' she said, 'and a pianist.' And a songwriter, though that wasn't an earner. When I told her I'd earned eleven dollars in royalties from APRA for a song, she said that was more than she'd ever earned on account of her winning song being stolen and released overseas.

The second string to my writing/teaching bow came about from research for a young adult novel. *Shreve's Promise* featured a teenage girl and a woman in her eighties. To gain a broader view of older people, I joined Age Concern as a volunteer visitor and completed a one-year certificate in care of the elderly. That job has helped me out over the years, when, as now, I live hours from a city, writing income is sporadic and teaching workshops far flung.

In my new life in Central Otago I applied for a job as a nurse aide in the rural hospital. There were so many applicants that five of us were given one permanent day each. To supplement my income I received a top-up from the jobseeker benefit from Work and Income NZ (WINZ). When I returned from a two-week job teaching writing in America and still couldn't increase my hours at the hospital, I found my benefit had been cancelled. I applied to have it reinstated.

'You'll have to come in for a video appointment,' I was told. The next week I drove forty-five minutes to Alexandra, walked in past the black-clad security guards to a small room where there was one other applicant, a young man who had been released from jail the day before. We sat together and watched a video that encouraged us not to take drugs, especially in the workplace, and told us of the benefits of making an effort to be employed.

'How are you getting on?' I asked him, when it finished. 'Have you got somewhere to stay?' He was tall, lean, dark-haired like my own sons.

'I'm at the campground. They put me up in a cabin.'

'Are you warm enough? Do you have enough blankets?'

'I have a sleeping bag, but it's cold.'

'You can go to the hospice shop, or the Salvation Army shop in town,' I told him. 'They have lots of cheap duvets.'

'Through the eyes of [Max-Neef's] Human Scale Development,' Emma Kidd writes,

> most of the social 'problems' we identify today, such as depression, alcoholism, eating disorders, unemployment, racial conflicts and dissatisfied youths, can be seen as *pathologies*. This means that, if we look carefully, each 'problem' can be traced back to an array of fundamental human needs which are not being met.

A woman came into the room to tell us we didn't qualify for any support today but must come back in a week and fill in forms.

A week later I again made the forty-five-minute trip to the office, walked in past the security guards, took the clipboard and forms I was handed and sat down next to a young man who turned out to be my friend from the week before.

'How are you doing?' I asked him. 'Did you manage to get a duvet?'

'The shop people were good to me. They gave me two duvets. They even gave me a radio.'

'That's great.'

'I never want to go back to prison again,' he said.

5.

It's quarter to seven in the morning and I'm making toast for two corridors of people. They lie in their beds in their darkened rooms, the sun about to rise over the Kakanuis. Their weary eyes are shut and the night is behind us all – the bells ringing for the toilet and the commode, for pain relief and a cup of tea and for the toilet again, which means they can't sleep. The wakeup calls are done for the midnight pills, the damp beds changed, the laundry folded, the dark corridors mopped, the handrails dusted, the toilets scrubbed and bathrooms cleaned. Now the radio is on, tuned to the local station – The Burn. Toast pops and I know what each person wants: marmalade or jam or Marmite, just butter or no butter.

There's something about the bright clattery kitchen with the tinny radio playing the Bee Gees and the smell of warm bread, about knowing what each tray needs, that as I turn to push down the lever on the toaster, bopping to the music, I realise with some surprise that this ease and sureness I feel in my work, in making breakfast for those who can no longer make breakfast, is joyous. How to describe it? It's not the job I wanted or yearned for; it does not compensate me well for the long nights with the alone, the dying, those who want to die, those who are afraid to die, those who will live a lot longer than they imagined or care to, and those who have stoically settled to life here, who will turn to me with a smile when I wake them for their porridge.

What is this happiness? It's brief, it lasts no longer than it takes to turn it over in my mind, than it takes to name it, this cocoon of music and light and simple tasks. A job that is needed.

The other aide walks in, ready for the morning shift. 'Oh good, it's you,' she says. It could easily have been another, who would rightly think the opposite. But we grin at each other and finish off the trays. I hold the door while she pushes the breakfast trolley through and up the long corridor, the teapot lids rattling over the bumps.

6.

I'm writing an application for a writing residency when the phone rings. It's my case worker at WINZ.

'Something needs to be done about you,' she says. 'You can't just shift here and sit on a benefit.'

I remind her that I have a permanent job one day a week at the hospital, and other shifts and teaching jobs as they arise. 'And right now, as it happens, I'm in the middle of a long application for a fellowship. It's about six hours' work to get one in.'

'You're always applying for something and it comes to nothing,' she says. 'You need to accept your writing is a hobby, because you don't make any money. We don't pay you to write.'

'And that is true,' I wrote to the manager at WINZ in Alexandra. 'WINZ pays me to survive until I am able to earn enough income by other means, with enough money to help pay for food and the mortgage, for which I am deeply grateful. The fact that I work at my writing at the same time as all the other jobs I do, paid and unpaid, and while looking for other employment, is a bonus. Having someone tell you that what you do comes to nothing is distressing.'

It was hard to be in this world and not desired, my mother told me. Not desired by her mother, her first husband, even her children sometimes, especially when we were teenagers.

'I'm fat, and a crabby old woman at times,' she said. 'But I always told you that you could do anything, and I believe it is still possible. I gave up on my art. I had too many hard things. My weight. I didn't have a voice for my music, and my song was stolen. One more thing taken from me. If I'd made it as a songwriter, where would I be now? Not in this old people's home.'

'You were a beautiful songwriter, and a talented pianist,' I tell her.

'Not now,' she says. 'I forget the music now. But I was.'

'Mum, just burn your bridges,' my oldest daughter said. 'You're trapping yourself by having an income from WINZ. Just stop it. Work will flow towards you.'

'Why did you even come to this district?' my case manager said at the next meeting. 'You should go back.'

Because my marriage ended, and my home was gone … Because I had to go somewhere … Because I wanted to be near my grandchildren … And back to where?

'The trouble with you,' she said, 'is you're too bright.'

After my appointment I walked out past the security guards, climbed into my car and cried.

I rang WINZ and asked to cancel my jobseeker benefit. 'I'm not walking through those doors one more time,' I said.

'You don't earn enough to go off the benefit,' the woman on the end of the phone said. 'You only have work one day a week. You won't get by.'

'No, but I ...'

I tried again the following week. 'I'd like to cancel my jobseeker benefit.' This time I did it.

In his book *Theory of Prose* Viktor Shklovsky wrote that art exists that one may recover the sensation of life. It exists to make one feel things, to make the stone stony.

David Shields wrote in *Reality Hunger*: 'There is something heroic in the essayist's gesture of striking out towards the unknown, not only without a map but without certainty that there is anything worthy to be found.'

7.

Due to staff illness I now have three shifts a week. On the morning shift after the breakfast run and the showers and dressing, cleaning begins. I enter the room of a man felled by illness in the night. His wife sits in the chair beside him. I greet them both and proceed to clean the basin and taps, first with a wet ribbed cloth, then polishing with a dry cloth until the enamel and taps shine.

'Everything has changed,' the man on the bed says. I turn with my cleaning cloths, the bag of rubbish.

'I know,' I say.

Later I bring them both a cup of tea and hold the cup to his lips. I lay his head back on the pillow.

'Everything has changed,' he says again. 'When you walked in the door, all my pain left.'

'It's true,' his wife says. 'He told me.'

'Oh,' I say, remembering. 'In my car, before I came into work, I said a prayer asking that all patients would be free of pain.'

Hopes, intentions, the energy you put out into the world, all mean something. I walked into a room to clean the basin, and the prayer I'd uttered came in the door after me, rolling up its sleeves. I'd forgotten the prayer. All I was thinking about was my cloths and hot water, but there it was anyway.

What does that mean for the thoughts, intentions, wishes we set loose in the world? Perhaps to be conscious of asking. Perhaps to trust in what we receive.

8.

Sometimes our whole world is comprised of meeting subsistence – as if subsistence is our main reason for living and not the springboard into joy and connection. Into understanding and participation. If what we do is not examined with a close eye, it becomes the dark well we draw on unintentionally; becomes the hard hand, the tears in cars, becomes the prison walls.

That desire to endure. Sometimes we need to unpick that and ask why, and why, and then how? Even if we don't know what our needs are, we know what they are not: exhaustion, frustration, sadness, despair. It is to sing we were made, not to endure.

9.

The time came to leave my hospital job. To trust that giving up night shifts, early morning shifts and the desirability of the fortnightly pay would open the time for writing. For idleness and artistry. To trust that I could rent out my room, teach enough workshops and sell enough stories to keep paying for my shelter. An unknown future. The Romantic poet John Keats described the ability to be in a state of unknowingness as negative capability. He thought it urgent for the poet's craft. Negative capability – capable of living with '*uncertainties, Mystery, doubts*'.

And then there is that wonderful essayist Edward Abbey, who, in the introduction to *The Best of Edward Abbey*, wrote: 'Each of my books … has been met with a sublime, monumental, crashing silence.'

What did I want to say? Not how hard this is, but how necessary.

What matters is to take responsibility for the source of joy. Not joy bestowed, but joy up-willed, like a thistle from the damp of earth. The sap constructing its own container. The white down lifting the seeds to air.

Growing Closer

When the suffering of another creature causes you to feel pain, do not submit to the initial desire to flee from the suffering one, but on the contrary, come closer, as close as you can to her who suffers, and try to help her. –Leo Tolstoy

THE GREENKEEPER had just boiled water for his cuppa when the rabbiter stooped at the door. He had two dogs with him, one a rough-coated huntaway, the other something more dangerous, white and sleek as a whippet.

'Off you go, get him!' the rabbiter said, before he even said gidday, and the dogs streaked off across the embankment of the bowling green where the rabbit liked to graze. The man poured water on his teabag. He lifted his mug but the rabbiter shook his head.

'Just had one down at the bakery,' he said. 'I'm going to get him sometime. Even if I have to shoot him myself.'

'You shoot that rabbit, I'll come after you with a gun.'

'Settle down. It's just a rabbit.'

'He's not hurting anyone.'

'Hah. The country's seething with rabbits.'

'Has he done anything to you? Dug up your carrots or something? He doesn't touch the green. He knows.'

'Jesus,' said the rabbiter.

'It's true. I've been here six years and the rabbit just as long. He only grazes the tops. He doesn't come down on the green.' The man put his mug on the table and sat down heavily in a chair. The rabbiter leaned in the doorway.

'There's been complaints.'

'I don't care.'

'Anyway, the dogs will get him.' They could both hear the frenetic barking, drawing away, coming closer, drawing away. A few minutes later the huntaway shouldered itself into the room and lay down, heaving.

'What else is happening?' the rabbiter asked.

'The grass is doing fine. Had enough rain. Sometimes that rabbit just sits up there and watches me.' (He didn't say its name. Waldorf, he called him – to himself, and sometimes to the rabbit.) 'He sits up there like he knows what's going on.'

'Josie must have him bailed up.'

The man pushed his chair back and went to the window. The second dog shoved against the door, came in panting and flopped down. The man kept his back to it. He held his hot mug in cupped hands.

'Next time, eh Josie?'

The man glanced back, saw the dog's muzzle was still white. No fur or gore. He tipped his head forward and sipped his tea.

Philadelphia. After the long flight and the crossing from winter to summer, from night to day to night to day, from writer to teacher, I walked out of the dimly lit dorm to the bright grass and stood barefoot on the lawn. The next night, sleepless and on Facebook, I would read that walking barefoot on the earth grounds you. A negative charge comes out of the soil and can cure you of anything from depression to asthma. Probably jetlag too. But I didn't know that then, and roamed around feeling the warm grass as something extra-terrestrial after all those shiny-floored airports. I went inside and put my shoes on and walked over to the library where I would teach. Later, I wandered down the stone-flagged steps to the secret garden with the stone angels, one a young girl whose arm hung, broken at the elbow, with a bird attached.

Last year I had lain on this lawn and written a poem that was not good enough to be shown to anyone. The way the leaves lifted and fell, my thighs on the grass. Now I stood in the dell looking up at the trees: one I didn't know, one a maple, one perhaps an oak. The grass starred with white flowers. A plant with silver-backed leaves and a cluster of red seedpods, growing in the sun between bushes. I plucked a twig of leaves and lay down on my shawl on the grass. I looked up at the trees, and I wasn't the same person as last year. I shut my eyes. Mostly the midges bit me. There were lumps of soil under the grass, small wormcast piles perhaps, knobbles of earth.

In the end the midges pushed me to get up and walk over to Gracemere, the 140-year-old three-storey house where we'd be giving readings. My eyes ached so badly I kept them shut as much as I could, walking on the soft nylon of the soccer field, almost staggering. I let myself into the back hallway of the house and into the kitchen, where I foraged like a bear for blueberries and strawberries before walking back, catatonic, to sleep again.

I once had a pig and her name was Clementine. She was a large white, which means pink, with a torpedo body and a playdough nose flared on the edges. We kept her in our front paddock, within the town boundary. Someone at work had asked, 'Would you like a piglet to raise for ham and bacon and sausages and pork?', all of which I ate, and we said yes. Until a letter from the council requested that we remove the pig illegally kept at 187 Bridge Street, Eltham.

Thursday was killing day at the works. I took time off at lunchtime, let Clementine out of the small wooden gate onto the road, for she always followed me, and walked down the road towards the freezing works. Twice she ran onto someone's lawn and set about digging it up with her elastic snout (as indeed she had ploughed up our whole paddock). Each time I ran in and shooed her out.

We came to the entrance of the works. Up the long driveway were yards crammed with sheep and beef cattle, and one with pigs who were crying out a high, screeching despair. Clementine, disturbed, began to run up and down the verge, squealing. Until that moment I hadn't questioned the idea that she would become roast pork with apple sauce. I stood on the verge under the sign, thinking what to do. I was stuck with an illegal pig, but I could not walk up that driveway with Clementine following me in all her innocence. I turned and began the long walk home. Clementine rushed ahead of me and waited, ran circles round my legs, ran again onto the neighbour's velvet lawn with her snout in the moss and clover, and finally back through the wooden gate into her paddock. Her fat pink hocks stayed her own, her shiny hooves weren't gelatine, her blood didn't become black pudding nor her head and ears soup, her tongue pickled and her shoulders crackling bacon. She nosed in the trough for the last of the half-eaten corn cobs then lay down on the dried earth in front of her trough, the sun on her harsh white bristles and pink skin. She shut her white-lashed eyes and I walked back to work.

I still ate meat that night, though not Clementine.

Carl D. Scott on a recent Facebook page:

> I have been inside about 15 NZ factory farms in the last few years. Pardon
> my language, but what I saw in those places f*cked with my head. And that
> takes some doing. I am not some naïve bleeding heart. I am an ex-freezing
> worker and ex-Army. Please believe me, those animals are not moderately
> uncomfortable. They are not slightly unhappy. Their lives are a living hell.
> And we kill over 100 million of them every year, just in this country alone.

In the morning I walk barefoot to the secret garden, grounding myself all
the way. Bright sun away from the maple's shadow. I rise and bend through
sets of Salute to the Sun, my legs so creaky I almost topple after round two.
I think of my partner's coercions when we're bike training. *One more time
one more time one more time*. I do it one more time. I don't know any of
the plants' names – ferns, rambunctious climber, plant with white spiky
flowers. The plant with red seedheads grows all the way up the stone wall of
the grotto. I walk down the steps to be nearer the marble angels and to say
a prayer – to be a good writer, to be a good teacher, for blessings on all my
family and friends and the man I love.

On the third day, with jetlag fading, I walk into the garden and am able
to take in shapes. Which plants are where. I climb broad shallow steps to
another level and see the trunk of the tree I had lain under the day before. I
hadn't connected the trunk to twigs and leaves, and now I do, approaching
it barefoot through a bed of ivy. It's a straight trunk, fine lines to the bark, a
cylindrical, deciduous tree. Though it's tall, it's younger than the other tree
whose leaves I'd watched flittering and turning and can now name: *oak*. The
oak's trunk is so old even the ivy climbing it is old, sewn on like boot straps,
and the bark so textured it is falling open. The oak supports three trunks
of ivy, and from these rise the swirl and loft of leaves. In the shadow of the
stone building, the maple tree.

The lawn is starred with white clover. There's a large root like a buried
log lying across the grass, which may be from the oak tree. The sky tufted
with white cloud shading grey in the centre, so that sometimes there's sun,
sometimes not. The wind skiffling the trees, the only sound one bird. Later,
in the kitchen at Gracemere, I show a plucked trail of leaves and green pods
covered in red hairs to a woman who knows gardening. She tells me this is
wild raspberry, Japanese wineberry.

In 1997 the haemorrhagic rabbit calicivirus was introduced illegally onto Central Otago farms in an attempt to kill off rabbits. 'It was just like snow around here, it was belly up everywhere, it was just absolutely magic,' farmer Donald Young recalled.

'That rabbit,' Digger Creighton said to me. 'It's true, it didn't ever dig up the bowling green. I was worried when I bought the house across the road. Retired there. But the keeper said, "That rabbit won't touch your vegetables. He might hop across and nibble a few of your roses, but that's all." I didn't believe him. In four years the rabbit didn't once bother me. You could see him, hopping round the outskirts of the green. Those dogs from the rabbit board gave it a good go. Every now and then the rabbiter turned up with them, but that rabbit knew every escape route. Then one day he was dead. Early one morning when the greenkeeper came to work, there was the rabbit. Dead in the middle of the bowling green. The keeper skinned him, cut him open. He wanted to make sure the rabbit had died of natural causes, put himself in the middle of the grass. And the rabbit must have done. There wasn't a mark on him.'

'The rabbit problem has escalated over the past couple of years to the point where we can confidently say we're losing the battle,' says farmer Gary Kelliher. 'The problem with poisoning is that people tend to rely on one tool. If you don't keep vigilant afterwards and combine it with follow-up work you can just end up back with your problem again.'

Wild rabbits. They're the scourge of Central Otago's dry hinterland, the ground moving with fur. And maybe every rabbit is a personality, capable of free choice, living within its own moral standards. I understand it's not my grass seething. It's not my lack of choice whether my crops are destroyed or not. But we are killing the rabbits slowly with a virus that blocks their organs. We are shooting them and running them into the ground with dogs.

'Through the process of paying focused and sustained attention [through Goethean perception] … we expand our field of empathy beyond our bodies to include the phenomena around us,' says Daniel Wahl in 'Zarte Empirie':

> It involves acknowledging our own personal involvement in how we
> usually meet the world, the fact that we all habitually employ a set of basic
> assumptions and concepts. We all have a history as observers and have
> formed ideas about the world, which influence what and how we perceive.

How we perceive a rabbit, for instance. According to one Australian website, 'The "humaneness" of a pest control method refers to the overall welfare impact that the method has on an individual animal. A relatively more humane method will have less impact than a relatively less humane method.' For instance, shooting a rabbit in the head entails less suffering than shooting it in the chest. Soft foot-pad traps involve more suffering, and even worse is to rip a rabbit out of its burrow. Rabbit calicivirus disease causes acute liver damage with resultant blood-clotting abnormalities. A slow death may result due to obstruction of blood supply in vital organs and/or internal haemorrhages. Calicivirus causes a lot more suffering than a shot to the head, though less than the foot trap. Inoculation with the virus causes the most suffering.

'When people tell me vegans are too extreme,' Carl D. Scott says on Facebook,

> I am reminded of the famous quote by William Lloyd Garrison, an American activist and journalist who was a strong campaigner for the abolition of human slavery. He was also told he was too extreme, and that he should tone it down … 'I will be as harsh as truth, as uncompromising as justice. On this subject, I do not wish to think, or speak, or write, with moderation. No! No! Tell a man whose house is on fire to give a moderate alarm; tell him to moderately rescue his wife from the hand of a ravager; tell the mother to gradually extricate her babe from the fire into which it has fallen; but urge me not to use moderation in a cause like the present. I am in earnest. I will not equivocate. I will not excuse. I will not retreat a single inch. And I will be heard.'

Here, sitting on a felled tree, the trunk now horizontal after being vertical all its life, the sawdust from its own wounds lodged in the bark. The air warm, sprinkled with the high voice of bird call. Clouds like small torn fleeces expanding and narrowing in the blue above. In the sycamore the leaves are a symphony of movement, chaotic and contained. The oak tree to be felled stands half-masted, a rope around its trunk, a pink X spray-painted on the bark. The men with chainsaws have gone to lunch. There is only this sun, this kind air, and the shadows of waiting trees.

I bring a cane of wild raspberry to class and place it on the table. Extra-sensory perception is an exercise of sustained and close attention to a phenomenon.

'Sixty observations,' I say, basing my exercise on the work of New Zealand herbalist Isla Burgess, of holistic scientist Henry Bortoft, and of Goethe, from whom all of this flowed. 'We'll go around and around the class.' Beneath the table our feet touch, linking us. We're all at one with this exercise.

'I see two leaves opposite one main leaf.'

'I see a cilantro shape to the leaves.'

'I see a red tinge on the stem.'

'I see leaves green on one side, pale mint on the underside.'

The longer and more deeply we look, the more the plant reveals itself to us – the fact that the small extensions are a finger length from node to leaf, and the branch is an arm length from base to top of calyx and fruit, a connection between our bodies and the plant's; and then beyond that, details like the small thorns that line the central vein of each leaf.

'I see the leaves are curling in the same direction.'

'I see at the top of the leaves, where they join the cane, the veins line up, but further down the leaf they don't.'

'I see that as the thorns grow bigger on each leaf, they keep the same distance between them.'

'The leaves sound like tissue paper, like birds' wings ...'

For the second phase, we shut our eyes and imagine the plant in all its phases. 'Exact sensorial imagination,' Bortoft wrote of Goethe's work, 'is to perceive the plant as an expression of the process of its own transformation.'

We imagine the wild raspberry from small seedling pushing out of the rough earth, to young plant, to the calyx covered in red hairs opening to the ripe ruby fruit, to the calyx left white and shrivelling after the birds and small insects have eaten their fill, the plant browning, the leaves curling back towards the earth and the vine-like branches settling into a season of snow and ice before the buds unfurl again.

'Attention without feeling, I began to learn, is only a report,' poet Mary Oliver writes. 'An openness – an empathy – was necessary if the attention was to matter.'

'Systematic practice of Goethean methodology,' says Wahl, 'will change our understanding of the nature of the material world, the nature of consciousness, and of our own human nature as conscious and *responsible* participants in and integral parts of Nature.'

One day my son said to me, 'If you're fighting for the rivers and against industrial dairying, why do you have cheese in your fridge? You're supporting Fonterra.'

'I have to give up cheese?'

'What do you think?'

At the end-stage of my parents' marriage we could no longer bring friends home to play. My brother and I didn't speak about this. We walked home from school on our own. We couldn't trust the sudden and sustained outbursts of shouting, or where they might lead. If I cried, I turned to my cat Tunku. I'd hold him close to my face, smell his warm-grass fur, rub my nose over his ears which were black and had the finest coating of velvet on them, like a horse's face. At night I'd fold his purring body into my chest. I never minded his fishy breath.

How simply and how often a child turns to an animal for comfort. We project our love, and our hunger for love, onto animals, and in return they recognise us as fellow creatures. Yet an animal is often under our power – unless it is a wild horse, for example, stepping forward, stretching out a nose, but with all the forest behind her to run to if she so chooses. We have every reason to benefit from all an animal gives us, but with this power come responsibilities – as a nurse would offer kindness to a patient with no memory and no voice; acts of unseen, unremembered kindnesses.

There are things right now that I'm not questioning because it suits me not to see them. And are there things that I don't know, which I don't realise I'm not questioning, and am therefore in a true but blessed state of ignorance? How much do I want to open my eyes?

What gives us domination is not our strength but the way we direct our minds.

In the garden the raspberry canes shine with a scarlet fuzz all over the fruit heads and the stems. The raspberry weaves its way through hay-scented ferns and a grape, enmeshed and yet thriving, supported and supporting in the greenery of others. There is a rightness of the plant in its own habitation. It doesn't grow limp and sparse under the gingko tree, but in the sun where all its needs are met, thrusting to life, wind-sheltered, its red globes spectacular.

The ability to see is to find the trunk of the tree whose leaves shelter me; tree as its own self, not just my shade.
The ability to see is to look for specifics so I might understand
a plant or creature is itself – not a genus, not a herd.
The ability to see is asking in a café if the cake is made with butter, and to say no,
instead of not asking, and then eating it.
The ability to see means illusions will dissolve, especially the ones that protect me
from knowledge and change.
The ability to see means watching the video where the calf is pushed down and a knife is slid across its throat, because this is what happens 2 million times a year in our country for us to have a thriving agricultural sector. And cheese.

One day at a rural café I looked up and saw, through the window, a dead shaggy-haired Highland steer hoisted upside down by one hoof in front of a tractor, which hauled it across the paddock. A second steer watched from the field as the farmer butchered its companion. In the cooling air the animal stood, face intent, among the lengthening shadows. The next day the paddock was empty of that steer as well. But I remember them, the one who went first, and the one who waited.

The ability to see means I understand that animals also see. They honour, by their attention, that to which we close our eyes. They stand in the grass in the mauve of evening, the air blood-scented, staring, long after we have gone inside and shut our doors.

The Primitive Hut

In the present rethinking of why we build and what we build for, the primitive hut will, I suggest, retain its validity as a reminder of the original and therefore essential meaning of all building for people: that is, of architecture. –Joseph Rykwert

MAYBE we all reach back in our hearts towards Roman engineer Vitruvius's primitive hut. I know I do – whenever I pass the relics of a goldminer's hut, a small tin hut or stone ruins, I turn my head. I've turned my head with longing for that type of simplicity ever since I was a teenager. But it is 'not enough to have a liking for architecture', as Marshal de Saxe wrote in the eighteenth century, 'One must also know stone-cutting.' I knew I would eventually have to build a hut for myself, and so I have – a mudbrick writing studio, around ten square metres, built without plan or consent or experience, and as lovely a dwelling as I could have imagined.

The hut sits to the north, facing the mountains, and in the sunlight is a tawny gold. Its red corrugated-iron roof matches the farm buildings in the valley and the houses in the village. It has white windows with small panes of glass in the north and east walls, a door in the north wall, and is built from 100-year-old bricks. Though we used string lines and level, the walls bulge and curve with the rumpty, pitted shape of the old bricks. My son Rory and I had taken down a mudbrick cottage a farmer wanted removed. That cottage was built in 1962 (proclaimed over the doorway), but the bricks themselves were from a much older building. We knew that, because inside the cottage the bricks were rain-pitted, uneven with age and weathering. The house beside that cottage was built in the late 1800s. Perhaps these bricks were from an earlier outhouse or storage room. The farmer didn't know.

At twenty to twenty-five kilos each, made mostly of a grey-brown loam and short tussock, flawed bricks sometimes collapsed as we carried them from wall to trailer. Yet in the walls the bricks' strength is unmistakable.

Horizontal snow and rain, and wind so strong that the branches of willows come loose across the paddock and bikes blow over – it makes no difference. Inside the hut it's calm and still. There's a queen bed with a patchwork quilt under the window, a bed so warm and wide and sun-filled that it's here I do my writing, propped against the mudbrick walls rather than sitting in the chair at the desk. Vitruvius's Triad, from his first-century book *De architectura*, required buildings to fulfil three qualities: *firmitas, utilitas, venustas* – that is, to be strong, useful and beautiful. My hut is all of these. It has its back to the wind and its eyes to the sun, and to see it arising from its girdle of tussock is to remember again the meaning and beauty of shelter.

We made the concrete floor by hand: two concrete mixers, two neighbours and Rory and I. Our first foundation turned out as pitted as the bricks, a rough cement surface. And now it glows with earth. I simply trowelled an earth plaster – three parts sand to one part sifted clay and one part fresh cow manure – over the concrete. With six coats of linseed oil the earth floor has deepened to a rich brown flecked with straw. Its surface is slightly undulating, as if I have run the curve of the palm of my hand over the earth, resting it in places. It is a floor that can be swept or washed – useful, beautiful and strong. And as John and Gerry Archer, the authors of *Dirt Cheap: The mudbrick book* wrote, 'for little or no cost'.

I bought *Dirt Cheap* in 1976, aged eighteen and newly married. Reading it again now I wonder what it was that set me off on a life believing in simple design and materials. Perhaps this quote: 'We found that many people were unaware of the exciting possibilities that exist when the limitations of conventional design and materials are removed.'

Vitruvius recommended:

a thrifty balancing of cost and common sense in the construction of works … the architect does not demand things which cannot be found or made ready without great expense. For example: it is not everywhere that there is plenty of pitsand, rubble, fir, clear fir, and marble … Where there is no pitsand, we must use the kinds washed up by rivers or by the sea … and other problems we must solve in similar ways.

In other words, by recycling – the door, the windows, the roofing iron, the bricks – and using what's around – the clay, the straw, the cow manure from over the fence. What if all architects strove to make use of the vernacular, things 'made ready without great expense'?

The north window beside the bed looks out to Mt St Bathans. A friend promised me that if I built the hut, he would take down the cracked willow across the paddock and give me a view of the mountain. Today, under sun and blue sky, it is burnished with snow. In a video made the day eleven people turned up to help with the bricking, beyond the sound of the concrete mixer turning is the sound of the chainsaw. There would be chainsaw whine, then a crash, then silence … I'd stand listening till the chainsaw started up again, friend Graeme safe, before turning back to the mixer.

Eleven people helping, seven of them over sixty, including five in their seventies. Rory had said to me, 'Mum, can you please find someone younger to help with the heavy lifting?' But it was mostly older people, intrigued and intrepid, who turned up to help, strangers and friends, as inexperienced as me but believing, as I did, and as our great-great-grand-parents obviously did, that we can build our own shelter.

One woman visiting from Scotland, Mary Cane, emailed to ask if she and her husband could help. They were an artist and a retired helicopter pilot in their seventies. I asked her why older people are the ones who turn up to help build. Because, she said, the older we get, the wiser we get, and we realise how right it is to build with earth. They couldn't lift the bricks up to the sixth and seventh courses and worked instead on the time-consuming job of preparing clay for the mortar. They dug clay out of my pile, sifted it through an old wirewove bedframe onto a sheet of corrugated iron, then tipped it into buckets.

With so many people helping, the bricks were layered up fast. I spent most of my time on the mixer making the mortar: four parts sand to two parts sifted clay to one part fresh cow manure and half a part of slaked lime. I'd mixed the hydrated lime with water in a drum the night before and loved its creaminess and texture, like white mousse, measured and tipped into the mixer as if I were baking.

On the lower courses of the bricks the mortar is in lumps and runs. I made the mix too soft and we didn't know enough to clean up as we went. By course four we had it figured out – a stiff mortar, and Brian making it his job to work with cloth and brush to keep the bricks tidy. And now they're brushed all over with a clay, lime and manure paint that unifies them: the bricks that are straight with the bricks that are weathered, the courses where the mortar ran riot with the courses where it is smooth. The walls, then, a record of our learning, our apprenticeship to earth.

I set out to prove it could be done, people building from the earth who didn't know how to build, for wouldn't this bring hope to others? I think of my son with wife and baby and a $400,000 mortgage. 'The cost of a thing,' wrote Thoreau in *Walden*, 'is the amount of what I will call life which is required to be exchanged for it, immediately or in the long run.'

Earth forgives – wet mortar or stiff, three parts sand or four, soil rich in clay or not. How did my bricks last 100 years with so little clay content? Someone dug and ploughed the earth where they lived and used that, and here the bricks are, in their third incarnation, a small beacon-of-hope-house, a slightly skewwhiff hut like a child's drawing: steep roof, window and door, and a person sitting outside in the sun, looking to the mountain.

Lifting Walls

ELSEWHERE in the country spring is blousy among the trees. Here in the Ida Valley it seems as if time stands still. The apple trees with their pink and white buds held tight among the slim arrowheads of leaves, the buds still clasped on their green wands, everything on the edge of blooming – the lilacs, the elderberries, the Santa Rosa plum tree. Surely today, I think, as I wander past the apple trees, but no. This is what it is to live in the coldest valley in the country, where snow can lie on the ground for seven weeks and spring hovers, like a diver jumping and jumping on the end of the diving board, arms upraised, while we wait and wait for that gorgeous leap and flight to begin.

Rain was forecast but it's not here by 5pm, and with the sun in its low arc towards Blackstone Hill the air is warm and still. I take a spade over to where I want to build a mudbrick wall. In this valley the winds are notorious for their velocity, and to grow food I need shelter, hence a farmer donated me bricks from a collapsed woolshed. A long line of mudbricks needs something to anchor it – either steel rods coming up through the bricks from concrete or, as I am planning, three fenceposts, with strands of barbed wire laid along the bricks to link them to the wooden posts and make the right-angled wall sturdy.

I've never built a wall, much less put in a fencepost. Graeme Male up the road told me he'd dug all his posts in without concrete, just ramming the earth around the post, which he thought gave a firmer job. With its separate components of gravel and cement, concrete has a different composition from earth and so can separate the post from the ground, he explained. But clay, shovelled into the hole, links cell to cell with the earth. I like any process that uses what is around me and requires no trips to town for cement, no extra days waiting for it to dry. Dig and tamp, that is all.

Brian has gone for a bike ride. Earlier he'd asked if I had any jobs I needed a hand with. I'd thought a bit and said, well, there are holes to be dug for the posts if you feel like a break from the screen. Now I want a break from the computer, from writing up the environmental society's performance report for the Charities Commission.

I think of ringing Graeme for advice. For instance, how deep should I dig, and how wide, and what would I use to tamp the soil? But I don't want to ask while the hole is still theoretical. Better to do some work first. Commit to the project. In the absence of knowledge or help, and with the mountains over my shoulder, the snow melting to rivulets that feed the clatter and burble of the Ida beyond the willows, I begin to dig. First the turf, cut in precise scoops, then into loam – which is a surprise, because sometimes when planting tussocks even in shallow holes I've had to use the grubber against rock and gravel.

In this patch of grass between the house and the mudbrick cottage, the land might once have supported a forest, the soil is so dark and friable. I have an instrument, a slim iron bar, pointed at one end, heavier with a weight at the other. I found it near the old shed on my property. It could have been made down the road at the historic Hayes Engineering Works, perhaps for this very task – plunging the pointed end into the soil and levering it, the point disturbing stones, breaking up hard earth. A few minutes work with the bar, and then with the spade, scooping dirt into the wheelbarrow. Plunging and scooping. I look up at the house and remember the first day of building when son-in-law Sam and I began the foundations like this, he moving ahead of me with the grubber and I following with the spade, scooping out the trench. Hour after hour, round and round in a trench the perimeter of the house, deepening and deepening, until by the second day, our hands burning with blisters, we had dug to the required depth of half a metre and could get on with the job of laying the concrete pad.

One hole isn't much in comparison.

The earth gives to the talking of the bar, and the wheelbarrow has to be emptied again and again, the hole so deep now it's hard to raise a spade in its narrow walls. I kneel down with the coal shovel and try lifting earth out that way, but my wrists aren't strong enough. Instead, I lean down into the hole and use my hands to gather soft, gravelly earth. With my face below the ground, I inhale the cool fragrance of earth, my arms stretched down into it in an intimacy. I am inside the earth, and an understanding comes to me in ways it doesn't when I walk upon it, unthinking, across the lawn or the rough clay work area where I make my plaster: that earth is not a surface but its own being. Bent over with my bum in the air, face down in the darkened chute I've dug, shoulders, elbows, forearms, wrists, fingers in contact with earth. It smells of minerals and cells, as clean and clear as a rockpool beside the ocean. Whatever decayed to make this soil has long disintegrated. It isn't the pungent almost-rot smell of leaf mould and humus in the top litter of forests, but bone clean. The days when only tussocks and moa inhabited this field are centuries gone, but they are here, as is the memory of the great lake that once covered these plains – water, then swamp, tussock, soil, stone. I want to say, hello my earth, my planet. I want to greet her in some way, eyes shut, head down, inhaling her. I think of Brian's poem 'Declaration':

> Without reverence
> for the world we inhabit
> we will never come
> to cherish the planet
> we depend on.

I had not thought of reverence when I came with my spade, only of my own tasks and concerns, my lists. Instead, I am humbled by wonder.

When I lift my head out, my hands full of stones, I see Brian stepping off his bike on one side of the house and Graeme climbing out of his car on the other.

'I was thinking of you both,' I say, and Graeme laughs.

'You summoned me again.'

Last week I'd struggled to unscrew a board on the bottom of the mudbrick cottage door. I couldn't plaster the floor until the door could be opened. I'd texted Graeme, *Do you have a drill bit for roofing screws I can borrow?* And then deleted the text and spent the next forty minutes searching for my own drill bit and watching YouTube videos on how to change a drill bit, because, as Sam taught me when we were building, look and look again before you ask for help. Rely on yourself to do things. But even though I'd deleted the text, Graeme called in anyway and helped me get the plank off the door. Now he arrives at my place just at the point of digging when I think I'm ready for the post.

'You must be a witch,' says Graeme.

'Good,' I say.

Both men come over to peer into the hole.

'Where did you bike to?' I ask Brian.

'Over Locharts Hill and down to the St Bathans turnoff. Head and side wind all the way back. I wanted to stop, but I said, "Fuck it, I'm not giving in."'

'I'll put that on your headstone, Brian,' I say. 'Fuck it, I'm not giving in.'

'He'll just be having a lie down for a bit,' says Graeme.

'And when we read it, we'll laugh again,' I say. 'If I die first, you can put it on *my* headstone.'

'Whoever goes first, the others have to have a bloody good party,' Brian says. That settled, we look back in the hole.

'That's deep enough,' Graeme says.

I lift the post and settle it into the hole.

'I'll hold it, you put six spadefuls of clay in – not the stony stuff you just dug out, clay from your pile. Clay's the closest material to cement.'

'I'll go home and get changed and come back,' Brian says, and bikes off.

I drop clay round the post.

'What will you tamp it with?' Graeme asks.

'My iron bar?'

'No, you need something thicker. I use a sledgehammer.'

I poke around in the shed for my son Rory's long-handled sledgehammer.

'Good. Now drop it down the hole, over and over.'

I drop it down, lift it up, raising my arms to give it height, half throwing it down the hole.

'Good. Keep doing that.'

Legs braced slightly apart, arms up, the weight of the steel hammer pounding the clay.

'Now get the level,' says Graeme. He holds it to the post while I add more clay, keep throwing the weight of the sledgehammer. Arms raised, I feel like Wonder Woman.

'When I was thirteen I had a holiday job with a fencer,' Graeme says. 'And old bloke. He taught me to do it this way, earth to earth.'

'And now I'm learning from you.'

A few years ago Graeme built me a dry-stone wall at the entrance to my house – a stacked-schist dry-stone wall extending for twenty metres with an entrance to one side. It's wide and safe enough for grandchildren to climb and walk upon. The one thing Graeme insisted was that we find the stone instead of buying it, a process that took many months.

'What is it about you and walls?' I asked Graeme over coffee one day.

'I've always observed stone walls in the landscape,' he said. 'I thought they looked great in a stark windswept land. Like in Yorkshire: no trees, just the pattern the walls made over the hills. They served a function, paddock-making. Out of all the built things humans have done that I've seen – St Peter's Basilica in Rome, the pyramids – it was those Yorkshire walls that captivated me. No need to go to the exuberance of building a cathedral. A stone wall will do it for me.'

The most difficult part of my stone wall, he told me, was finding the right stones – even though the land here is full of stone. They had to be top-and-bottom flat and a variety of sizes and thicknesses.

'I wanted to build with haphazard sizes. If you eliminate regularity, you take away any hint of a manufactured process – even the strawbales came out of a baler irregular, and your old mudbricks are a bit irregular. Not conforming to manufactured size was key to the look of the wall.'

Mine was the first dry-stone wall Graeme had built. He hadn't been taught, but looked up YouTube videos on how to go about it.

'I knew I needed solid foundations and through-stones to bind the wall. I knew what I wanted to achieve.'

The basic form of stone walls in Central Otago, I read in Jill Hamel's *The Archaeology of Otago*, is that of the Galloway double dyke:

> two carefully placed layers of stone on each face rising from a broad base to a narrow top with long, side-stacked capping stones on top, and a rubble fill in the centre. Long 'through' stones should be placed at regular intervals about 60cm above the ground surface to tie both sides together …

Graeme and I had walked on the rail trail searching for rocks that had fallen from the chiselled banks, and neighbours Pete and Jo Ryan had a stack of stones under a hedge on their property. There Graeme found some the right size. Over one metre, he placed the large flat stones as a template.

'I knew it was going to work, then. I just had to keep going, keep finding the right stones.'

He and I travelled back-country roads, up to Falls Dam and Danseys Pass with friend Declan and a trailer. Mike Tudor gave us offcuts from

nearby Pennyweight Quarry and told of stones where a stream feeding the
Maerewhenua Stream crosses the Danseys Pass road. Heaving the stones,
some of them a metre long and fifteen centimetres deep, became Graeme's
personal journey.

'I was coming out of cancer medication, which took all of my energy for
a year and a half, my testosterone blocked. It took me another year to get an
inkling of my strength, and that was the building of the wall. I regained my
strength through exertion.'

In May Sarton's poem 'Lifting Stone' I found an echo of that process:

> To build a pyramid or clean bright wall
> ...
> What soars is always buried deep for ages,
> Gently explored in the hill's dark mind,
> Prized, hewn in slow, thoughtful stages
> ...
> ... a figure standing there alone
> Whose work, humble and hard, is lifting stone.

'Being a stone-wall builder,' Graeme told me, 'makes me feel more
connected to the march of humanity, from apes to when we become extinct.
Millions have built stone walls before me and millions will build them after,
and I've taken my place in that lineage. It's a mark of my humanity. The
stone is important to me. It could be my Yugoslav background: everything's
rocky, you build your homes and your fields with stone. With this wall, I've
taken my place with my ancestors.'

Here in Central Otago the paddocks are rarely lined with stone walls. The
small villages have their walls – Ophir, Clyde and St Bathans, for example.
But in the fields, and without timber, the farmers worked with what was
plentiful and quick, and that was sod. Sods were generally cut from long
strips down either side of the wall, writes Hamel:

> and stacked upside down in five to eight layers. Each sod was cut with
> a sloping cut across the short ends, and a properly made wall showed a
> herringbone pattern on the face as each layer of sods was stacked with the
> angles alternating to the layer below. The sloped ends allowed each relatively
> fragile sod to pack down against its neighbour ...

But with their unprotected tops, sod walls did not last in Central Otago. Drought and frost prevented plants from growing in the exposed soil and the walls gradually dissolved back into the ground. If only tussock had seeded along the sods, how beautiful would have been the wind-tossed walls.

There are still traces here, an engineer told me. If you know how to look, you can sometimes see a line, a shadow, running straight across a paddock.

In coastal Otago with its warmer and wetter climate, Hamel writes, sod walls became covered with gorse, tussock and fern and are well preserved, sometimes to their full height.

Seven and a half mudbricks – that's all it would take for a row in my wall.

I saved making the mortar till the grandchildren arrived, especially ten-year-old Indy. When we were building the mudbrick hut she'd said, 'Grandma, I want to help,' and had knelt with me on the floor with her own bucket of mud, straightening the mortar.

On this particular day she watched me sift clay for a while then took over the whole operation: heaving the wirewove bedframe onto a sheet of corrugated iron, using a grubber to loosen the clay from the pile, digging it out into her bucket then spreading it on the wirewove. She pressed and shook the filigree of springs until the fine dirt fell through, then lifted the bed off. She knelt with the coal shovel to scoop up the sifted clay, 'like gold' one natural plasterer had told me.

Sifting is the process that holds everything up. Sand is delivered by the truckload (unless I've run out, in which case I walk across the paddock to the stream for some), and lime by the sackful. Collecting cow manure takes a bit of wandering through the paddock with bucket and spade, as grandsons Phoenix and Sonny had done with me earlier, but the results are fun and fast. Sifting the clay is a pedantic job. Often my mind sifts, too, over past regrets and choices, but looking across at Indy, industrious and proud of her strength, I felt grateful for her companionship and ownership of my onerous task.

At the concrete mixer I tipped in the buckets of clay, the pearly sand, the green stenchy cow manure, the perfect luminescent lime. Then it was a matter of waiting and waiting as the mixer turned. If I tipped in too much water before the lime had smudged into the clay, I would end up with a mix that smeared itself around the drum and had to be scraped out by the handful. I called Indy over.

'See that mix,' I said. 'It's flumping around heavily and some of it has clumped into balls. It's too dry.' I tipped in a cup of water. Another cup. Stood back and watched the action change. Another cup. The plaster began to move as one load, peeling off the top of the bowl as it turned.

'Look up the top there,' I showed Indy. 'It's flowing like a waterfall as it turns over. That's how you want it to look.'

The next day, snow.

'Were you ever nervous?' I asked Graeme.

'I had a sureness; I was absolutely convinced the stone wall would work. Choosing and placing the stones wasn't done at an intellectual level. It was at a physical, organic, body level. And I didn't ever become defeated. It depends how much patience you have, to lay some stones down and take them away again. Patience, and your commitment to the final wall as you imagined it. That's it – imagination and patience. And taking the time the job needs.

'It was a dream come true – a lifetime dream for me. You can follow your instincts in the form of wish and dream, and it can come true. A small wall doesn't have to be a big dream. It's nothing else but a wall. It's not trying to be anything clever. And when I see it now, it's absolutely perfect. It's not just for one person, like when I was painting. It's for you, the kids, for people in the village to see. It's a community artefact. In 100 years some local historian, like Judy Beck, will need your story to know who built the wall.'

One morning I stood outside with thoughts of all the jobs needing to be done. I felt capable only of the most basic of tasks; something as quiet as walking alone, as untaxing as folding clothes. It was warm in the spring air, and no wind. I could sift clay for mortar, a simple job needing just dirt, a bucket and my hands. I didn't want the heave of a corrugated-iron sheet and wire springs for sifting, only a sieve. My mind was overwhelmed with thoughts, dilemmas, anxieties. I walked over to the dirt as if to the doctor.

The new, round green sieve I recently bought fitted closely on top of a twenty-litre bucket. I dug out clumps and crumbs of clay from the clay pile, lifted a shovelful onto the sieve, then squatted next to the bucket and shook the sieve. Fine particles of clay fell through to the bucket. The clay was dry and workable, and the lumps left in the sieve broke apart easily in my fingers. For a few minutes I crouched there in the sun, holding and crumbling each lump till it fell through the mesh. Those that were too hard I tossed away into the long grass over the bank. Shovelled more clay onto the sieve. Crouched and began again. Not much to think about except my hands and the soil. The way the particles shifted and sorted. The way the depth of soil grew in the bucket. The heat of the sun on my shoulders. The balls of my feet pressed into the ground.

Balance, continuance, strength.

The making of mud gives you all of those things. Ah, the simplicity of labour.

Scottish writer Nan Shepherd wrote, 'There is a deep, pervasive satisfaction in these simple acts. Whether you give it conscious thought or not, you are touching life, and something within you knows it.'

And, as always, there was silence, only the intermittent chitter of birds and the faint clatter of the stream.

There's a moment in carrying a mudbrick over to the wall when I realise wall-building has become natural for me – as easy as mowing lawns. My arms carry the weight close to my chest. I lower the brick into a baby-bath of water: a wet brick will bond with wet mortar with less cracking. I take up the bucket of mortar and begin to smooth handfuls along the top of the last row. I no longer miss all the workers around me, or need any help, or feel anxious that I'm doing something wrong. My hands judge the depth of mortar and my eye chooses the next brick, judging the height and width. I no longer use the level. Now and again I step back and look along the row, then return to my task. I lift the water-soaked brick out of its bath, the water running down my wrists, and carry it over to the wall. I place it on the wet mortar, push it back into the previous brick to straighten it, then press more mortar into the gaps between the new brick and the lower course. The mortar is thick like biscuit dough, a light brown. My hands push and smooth at their task, and when it's done I walk back to the pile to choose another brick. Step by step the wall gains another layer. Out of interest, I take the long red level and place it on the wall – the spirit bubble settles right in the middle. I move the level along to the next section – the same again. I smile to myself and take the level back to the shed.

Some of the bricks are jagged and I've made them square with handfuls of mortar and stones off the driveway, or thrown broken chunks of mudbrick onto a rock then taken the smaller fragments and pushed them into the mortar. A mosaic wall. And straight all the same.

These bricks are over a hundred years old. I'm happy to make something new from them, preserving the work of the unknown brickmakers of last century. Even the ruined, crumbled bricks I found a use for, tumbling them into the garden and planting potatoes in their ancient glacial silt.

There's no wind at all. It's hard to believe after yesterday's gale, the wind so chilly I stayed inside all day though my hands longed to be smoothing mud. It's a blue-sky day, an abrupt summer day, the snow almost all gone from the Hawkduns and the Ida Burn singing with snowmelt.

'There's so much green,' a cyclist had said to Brian and me at Hayes Café at lunchtime. 'Forget fifty shades of grey, its fifty shades of green.'

'I know. It's weird,' I said, 'though it'll turn to brown for sure.'

She told us how her group had stopped on the rail trail near a tunnel, where one of Brian's poems is printed on a plaque, and she'd called to her friends to listen while she'd read it out.

'I read it slowly, with feeling,' she said.

Spring again. I've finished another wall. A community artefact, as Graeme put it. Perhaps, after me, someone will treasure these walls, care for them. Or perhaps they will grow potatoes from their rubble. For now, I have the beauty of the sun on their sides, the usefulness of their sheltering arms.

I think of how walls hold our memories.

I know when my friend Polly died: between the fourth and fifth layer of the first wall.

I know that on the sixth layer I worked in the snow laying bricks. The grandchildren, Indy, Phoenix, Sonny and Lucia, with their faces to the window, watching. Too cold for them to come out, me too driven to go in. To use and not waste the mortar. To see the wall through.

I know that on this third wall, at the fourth layer, my twelve-year-old Australian granddaughter Lacey walked to me with a ten-kilo mudbrick in her arms. How she said, 'Grandma, I think I could build a house of bricks.'

This spring, frost came again at budburst. The plum blossoms and some of the apple blossoms are burnt brown. Some trees won't come to harvest, but the crab apple tree I planted for Polly is in its tentative first-year flush of pink. The new lilac is flowering, purple, sweet, and reminiscent of my grandmother who picked bunches in spring for her table.

I think I am finished with the building of walls. Now my job is to protect them: to keep up a render of clay and lime on the southwest flanks, to renew the lime plaster capping when it needs it. In their shelter this summer I'll plant tomatoes, beans, courgettes. Already there is miner's lettuce, beetroot and kale, those hardy survivors. In the chinks of the garden I leave the dandelion and chickweed be. They are foods too, wild, freely given. Bright buttons of yellow, delicate petals of white against the rugged earth.

What if a River Wants to Sing?

IN THE UPPER REACHES of the river, it is the river's voice I feel with my skin, my cheeks, my ribs, my heart. For the water knows nothing of what is to come, only from where it has come – waterfall, spring, stream, cleft – to this, a ripple/tumble so vociferous and glassy and light-filled, so clattery and fresh, that to step into its wild push is to feel as if I, too, have come from gleam of snow and will end in the wide surge of sea.

There is no-one alive who has seen the Manuherekia River as it once was, flowing with its own strength from beneath the Hawkdun Range and Mt St Bathans to where it slides into the Clutha/Mata-Au at Alexandra. Since the days of gold we have cut channels and leaked the river's water away, so that in places it turns from tumbling alpine river into stream, from glassy waves to sluggish and shallow. On the banks the lucerne and choumolier thrive; on a farm bridge over the river a black and white dairy herd ambles to pasture. In the green fields, now denuded of beech and tussock, pivot irrigators turn and cast water upon ryegrass. And at Alexandra, where the beloved water slurps around knees, holds torsos and arms in warm, willowy afternoon haze, few are aware of the river's spangly beginning or its possibilities.

And that is why, in January, a group of scientists – freshwater ecologists and a hydrologist – have come to walk beside the river, to count each step of run, riffle and pool, to note each habitat, to be with the river along its length. We begin our first walk in the middle section of the river while flows are still reasonable.

'We should have been doing this every year for the last seventeen years,' one scientist says. 'We were always told the upper reaches were fine. And they *looked* fine, at the key points we drove to. But we didn't know the impacts on the river over its length. I mean, a river this size shouldn't look like this.' Water silent of mayfly dance and hatch rising, of trout swirl, of the quick flick of native galaxiids, of its own joyful voice. The rocks next to the river are coated in fine silt, baked white in the sun and grim to look at. Days later, when it rains and we are still walking, our feet slide on the slippery surfaces. In the shallows the stones are gauzed with long, filamentous algae. Green strands slip through the water. The brown-coated stones are treacherous on the edge, and in the middle of a swift rapid, the water piling against knee and thigh, the rounded rocks under my boots offer only slidiness, a moment of fear. The river has changed.

We don't know the river's true magnificence. We also don't know the lowest threshold at which the water and all the water creatures can survive and thrive. But the day of reckoning is near. On 1 October 2021 a number must be conjured – from the steps we count, and from the hydrologist, the ecologists, the planners, the economist, the community and the social impact studies – to establish a minimum flow: one that enables people to take water for various purposes and still allows aquatic ecosystems to thrive and the river to retain its natural character.

In 1865 water rights were granted to people for goldmining. These mining permits were not subjected to any minimum flow regulations. They were titled to the land and became deemed permits for farmers. Now, instead of sluicing the cliffs and hillsides to reveal gold, the water soaks the land. Whole communities are built around this.

But the river is calling us to account.

Today there are four of us on the walk beside and in the river: two water ecologists and two poet-environmentalists – Brian Turner and I. We start from the St Bathans Loop Road bridge, high up near Falls Dam. For the first few hours of walking the river accompanies us with its tumbling and rushing in long stretches of ripples. The air is mineral scented from the wet rocks and water sparks. The rocks are slabby sandstone and rounded river boulders. On the banks grow tussock, briar rose, thistle, broom, buttercup, bugloss, woolly mullein and rushes. In the warm air their fragrance rises. The yellow flowers of buttercup thread through briar and grass, the bugloss that turquoise purple/blue, and the tussocks sing of how the land once was – golden fields of snowgrass, not this pasture that stretches away from the braided gravel banks to roll over the hill.

'Come on! Come on!' a voice yells, and on the other side of the river sheep pour over a slope. Two pied stilts rise up calling from the stones and fly into the sky, which is grey with patchy low cloud. The river grey too, over grey stones, and only the wildflowers weaving their brightness along the banks.

One scientist is long-legged and young and strides ahead along the riverbank. The older scientist, whose turn it is to count and record every step he takes for the habitat assessment, stops to write figures and looks about at the braided fields of gravel.

'Under the water plan,' he says, 'the river's natural character has to be protected. This is good up here, so far. The Clutha above Lake Dunstan is good, too, but below the dams there's hardly any of the natural character left.'

He tells us the Manuherekia is running at over 2.5 cumecs, or cubic metres of water per second. That this is enough to maintain the river's health is evident by the ripple and roar of the flow, and by the clean stones, the clear water – so free of nutrients that he finds the cotton-wool balls of didymo on rocks. Didymo is an invasive algae, one that threatens insect life and makes slimy and slippery the rock substrate of a river. It's a species that doesn't like excess nutrients, however: further downstream where the river is slower and runs through farmland, there'll be no didymo. 'It doesn't like phosphate,' he says.

He begins to step and count again. Ahead, the younger scientist stops where a small tributary burbles into the river and records the water temperature. 'Sixteen degrees,' he says, adding that temperatures above 19.9 degrees Celcius are stressful for some invertebrates. We splash through a wide shallow ripple. Pied stilts calling. The sluiced cliffs tan and gold.

I come to a swift river crossing. The young man is far ahead and I didn't see the route he took. In the rapid the water is deep and clear and rugged over the rocks. Brian and the ecologist are standing by a pool discussing fish numbers. I don't want to ask either of them where I should cross, or how. If I were here by myself I would have to figure it out. I step into what looks the shallowest but fastest segment. The water piles against my knees. My boots slip, one then the other, and I pause, unsure, the water mid-thigh, my arms outstretched for balance. The two men have entered upstream from me where the water is slower, not so deep. My path is like horizontal rock climbing – the pause to find each foothold while the river, warm and glassy, surges against my thighs. It's a relief to reach the shallow edge again where the water laps the stones.

After four and a half hours we stop for lunch on a grassy bank. We take our boots off, empty out the pebbles, wring out our socks and lay them on the hot stones. The river sings by, rippling into a pool.

We set off on our walk again, the river beside us deepening in the riffles. The substrate is of smaller cobbles and the flow not so swift.

'I've seen twenty goats so far,' the younger scientist says. I thought I smelt something strangely sweet in the air. I'd bent to smell the purple thistle on the riverbank, thinking it was that. I'd seen deer hoofprints, though. A large stag, the older scientist thought.

'We flew over here with a hydrologist a few years back,' he tells us, 'and there were at least 300 deer on the riverbank.'

'Why were you in a helicopter?' I ask. 'Wouldn't it have been better to walk?'

'He was a key hydrologist, expensive. It was a better use of time to fly in and out of points to check. The hydrologists would like flow sites on every tributary, measuring and sending flow data electronically. They'd like forty years of data on the river to set a minimum flow. We've got two to four years of data, and this is a complex river. We've got no data before 1920. We don't know the natural river.'

I wade the river beside the young scientist, his long thighs above the water. He hardly pauses in his talk as we negotiate the flow.

'Once I was working with a PhD student,' he tells me. 'We were crossing a river and he stopped in the middle and said, "I can't go on." The water was pulling at us. A big wide powerful river. I said to him, "You can do it. I can tell you a few things that will help."'

'Can you tell me those things?' I ask him.

'Sure. Make sure you're crossing on an angle slightly down-river. Go with the flow instead of struggling against it.'

I don't know why this had never occurred to me. I recalled the earlier crossing, stuck halfway across the river and attempting, if anything, to walk slightly upstream.

'Second thing, don't put your foot straight down on the rocks. Feel your way with your boot. Lower it towards the substrate, then let the river guide your foot down the last inch. It's like skiing, sliding along the rocks.'

'River skiing,' I say, trying it out.

'That way, you know you're safe once you do put your foot down. And the third thing: if the going gets tough, wedge your boot in between rocks. Let the river wash your boot into place.'

I slide my boots through the water. For the next few crossings he stays beside me, not reaching for my arm to steady me, but his presence just downstream from me a reassurance.

'There you go,' he says, as I make the shallows.

With the low cloud it's hard to read the depth of the water before entering. We cross upstream of ripples and angle slightly downstream. The flow is warm and rushy on my legs. There's a harsh cry of a heron, long strutty body up ahead on the bank. It stands beside unruffled water, while the willows near me toss in a silent wind I cannot feel.

The day before, the first day of the river walk, we negotiated one of the lower sections from Chatto Creek to Shaky Bridge, a long nine-hour day on the river. An open invitation to walk the river with the scientists had gone out to all those concerned with the river – the mayor, regional and district councillors, water users, their advisory contractors, Fish & Game and those in the community concerned about the Manuherekia. It's early morning, the sun just rising when we gather on the riverbank above a blue and shiny river: three scientists, a Fish & Game officer called James and me. I don't know any of them and wonder how I'll cope, particularly with the river crossings. I'm still affected by concussion and a sprained elbow from a riding fall. The concussion has challenged my talking and my balance. I think I'll be okay if I concentrate on every step, like the hydrologist who is counting and recording steps today. And plod. I know how to plod.

But I am frustrated that those charged with the responsibility of making decisions about the river aren't here, nor those who argue their right to the water. To know the river, that is the thing. I think of the plea made by New Zealand acclimatisation societies when they applied for a protection order on the Ahuriri River: 'The scenic qualities of the Ahuriri cannot be adequately conveyed in words … or photographs,' their application read. 'It is hoped that the tribunal members will visit the river to form their own opinions.'

The sun casts our shadows across the stones. It's a clear morning, the stones bright, snow on the Old Man Range ahead of us and the river wide, defined by the scrawls of willows on each bank. I slide my legs down into the water, which is deep and cool, and follow the four men out onto the opposite gravel bed, my boots soaked for the day. Bird chitter in the willows, ripple of water, snatches of conversation.

I could ask questions, but I'm content to listen. 'Something's not right,' the older scientist says. The river's meekness, and places where the water is murky and slow under broken trees, as if we are in the bayou. We round a bend and splash through a shallow thirty-metre-wide riffle over bronze cobbles. Our boots send up sprays of light.

'All I know is that there's not enough water in the river,' he says. 'For the minimum flow, we shouldn't be starting with a number and working backwards to prove the river can sustain it. We should start at the beginning and use scientific processes to get a number for the river. Last year, with low flows, irrigators were taking a high percentage of the river: 213 water takes, 700 customers. We need to work together, all of us. Farmers, protect the river from your stock. Trout anglers, give up some space for native fish, they're becoming extinct. We have to protect them.'

We cross and re-cross the river. I count the birds I see: fourteen pied stilts, ten paradise ducks, ten mallards, one duck dead on the riverbank, one hawk cruising above. A river smell of wet willow leaves, drying silt and algae, water on rock. Closer to Alexandra thyme perfumes the air. On the gravelly tracks beside the river the pungent twiggy thyme, woolly mullein with its grey velvety leaves, broom.

On the last kilometre-long stretch to the bridge the river is shallow, its wet width as wide as its banks. We walk in single file up the middle following the thalweg, the centre line of the river. It's a cobbly path we're on, the water over the tops of our boots. The blue sky has turned grey with low cloud and a bitter wind reminds of snow on the ranges. Plodding, one splashy step after another. My sore arm tucked into my shirt for a sling. In the willow branches overhead the sparrows sing.

Ways to describe a river: run, riffle, (rapid) cascade, pool, backwater, glide (shallow, rapid, deep)

Ways to describe the substrate: bedrock, boulder, cobble, pebble, gravel, sand, silt

Ways to measure a river: count every step of run, riffle, pool. Measure the depth in twenty places at multiple cross-sections. Measure the wet width, the velocity, the riparian cover. Measure the temperature of tributaries as they enters the main stem. Measure the temperature of the main stem. Measure the nitrogen, the phosphorous, the faecal bacteria. Measure the clarity, turbidity, suspended sediments, the dissolved oxygen, the pH, the macroinvertebrate community, the fish species, the connectivity – for instance, does the river flow all the way from source to receptive body of water? Does the river flow?

It is not just the sights – an unexpected deep and limpid pool, a jewel-like blue/green beneath white limestone cliffs where wild pigeons have enlarged narrow cracks into small dark homes that look out from the cliff-face like eyes, and the willow tree shading the riffle that feeds the pool, the water ruffling and tinkling over the cool stones and becoming almost still. These are place-markers on the way. But it is holding the river in one length in my mind that brings respect. From standing in the waters at the confluence of the east and west branches high up under the Hawkdun mountains, feeling the east water slower, warmer on my right thigh, the west branch swift and cool on my left thigh. Following the river from those clear alpine beginnings. The power of the water as I ford it, feet slipping on boulders, through the long length of braided strands where the pale, dried-silt-covered rocks glare in the sun and the way seems interminable to the far willows. The river each side clattering, gliding, making forays towards itself in shallow wide ripples, joining one braid then parting and rejoining, singing all the while, flowing silent behind townships, hidden behind willows and rucked paddocks of cows, behind Lauder and Becks and coming out at Ōmakau in pools and ripples beneath the bridge, the last pool deep to my thighs, the water warm, the rocks still slimed under my boots. And then the river turns through the valley again, that sequence of riffle, glide, pool, over and over, each bend bringing a new vision of light on water and the continual voice of the river, rushing and clattering. Or the times of peace, quiet enough in a glide to hear quails snickering, or to watch a single blue heron turn and soar on outstretched wings and come in to land on stones. The river broadening, becoming one wide stretch between willows, water shallow over brown stones, the edges thick with silt and algae.

Sometimes the river narrows to a stream after a water intake. There are bulldozed ramparts where man has assured himself of his own plenty.

Map for the heart

Then as each tributary clatters in, the river grows again. Beyond the willows the pivot irrigators turn and spray, and between the willows, in braids and pools, the river makes its way. There's a smell of wet silt and algae, the beginning rot of things.

Under Shaky Bridge where the townspeople come to play, the Manuherekia, brown, shallow, is their river. There are children in small plastic boats, a young man standing in the shallows. Another man on a motorbike rides up the middle of the riverbed, past the bathers and toddlers, wheels churning the stones, and disappears around the corner, the throb of motor fading.

I have seen the river at its beginnings, at the tributaries falling silver from the mountains – the Ida Burn, Rocks Creek, the Dunstan. I have seen the wild shags on rock cliffs, the dart and joy of young fish in clear pools over clean stones, and felt the surge and thrust of the stream through stretches of tussock and rock, over boulders that glisten golden or white pierced through with green. In the wide expanse of tussock lands and through rocky valleys the streams come to the river. I hold in my mind the whole length of the Manuherekia. To know the river like this, each step of it; to be beside it, to merge with the water, to be in its ripple and sing, hour after hour after hour, is to know one thing and that is this: the river is its own being and, as such, has the inherent right to thrive.

Trees that once grew here: mataī, miro, tōtara, beech

Fish that are endangered: Central Otago roundhead galaxias, alpine galaxias (Manuherekia), Clutha flathead galaxias, kōaro, tuna/longfin eel

Streams where moa-hunting tools were worked: Little Bremner Creek, Hills Creek (porcellanite, silcrete)

Birds that once lived here: moa, kiwi, kōkako, South Island saddleback/tīeke

Birds that are endangered or at risk: black-fronted tern/tarapirohe, wrybill/ngutuparore, South Island pied oystercatcher/tōrea, pied stilt/poaka, banded dotterel/tūturiwhatu

Tell the unspangled truth, says memoir writer and teacher and Beth Kephart. And I want to, about our river. For today, when we walked the Manuherekia at a one-cumec flow, less than half that of the previous walk, the wonder has gone. There is no magic about the next corner or the next ripple pulling at our legs. From the rail bridge near Chatto Creek I see that the main river has shifted from its former channel. Now a group of us stands on a dry river bed with tumbled boulders. A month ago, crossing here on my first day of walking the river, a scientist had seen me attempting to roll my shorts further up my legs. 'That's not going to do you any good,' he'd said, and I'd just had to slide into the deep water, right here, over these baked white boulders, and wade through, the water cool to the tops of my thighs.

Now the river is over by the opposite bank, favouring its smaller braid, moving dankly under the willows. We cross the boulders towards it. Morgan Trotter, from Otago Fish & Game, turns over a large rock in the dry stem. Underneath, two damselfly larvae scribble. 'They're big enough to have survived so far,' Morgan says. He looks around and points to the pawprints of a wild cat in the still-damp silt. 'Cats would have eaten any fish stranded by the river shifting. They'll be eating these damselfly nymphs too. Once we set up a time-lapse camera on a river that was dropping. There were certainly plenty of fish stranded on the rocks by that event, but when we came to the river, the fish were all gone. The cats get them.'

Matt Sole, an archaeologist and member of the Central Otago Environmental Society (COES), looks around at the boulders. 'I swam here regularly over the summer and autumn months through the 1980s,' he says. 'I've never seen it empty like this.' It was shocking, the dry exposed boulders, the defined channel stretching ahead of us, the force of the water gone.

We follow the limpid remaining channel: three of us from COES (Matt, Brian and myself), the water ecologist from Otago Regional Council, Morgan from Fish & Game, a farmer called Hamish (the only water-user to come on the river walks), and Christine from Landpro ('Make the most of your land').

We cross ripples ankle-deep, the water not even wetting my boot laces, and wade through glides up to our shins. I stop in one and stand there. The water still flows past my legs, but of the water's presence, its muscly strength, there is nothing. It is a river you cross without halting your talk, without stopping to consider the safest place to enter. Boots still slip on the cobbles and rocks. You can see the fine coating of algae across the riverbed, sometimes the matted back poisonous variety. Slip, slip on the stones, but no push back from the river. It smells of algae, has a brownish tinge, an insipid flow.

The silt fills and packs the interstitial spaces between the rocks and stones where the invertebrates make their homes. It carries its load of nitrate, phosphate, bacteria and toxic chemicals into our living waters. Thick algal growth leads to wide daily fluctuations in pH and oxygen levels, affecting the small creatures and degrading the river in its biology and beauty.

We come to the Galloway irrigation intake, where two-thirds of the already depleted river has been shunted off to the side by bulldozed banks. We know it is two-thirds because the hydrologist, who is waist-deep measuring cross-sections of the channel, tells us. Over to the right the main stem of the Manuherekia limps on. I cross it in two steps. All that consent asks of the irrigation company is that a river fifteen centimetres deep and thirty centimetres wide is left for the public's recreation.

Christine walks ahead of me through the shallows. It's her first river walk. In the upper reaches I'd had to stop in the middle of the river, unsure of my next step. Here the river seems like nothing more than a utility for human convenience. I wade through the shallows and onto the silted stones, my head aching and a feeling of loss and sadness all through me. One foot after another.

'I'm just getting to learn about this river,' Christine says. 'But – it's not a *terrible* river.'

Is that the most we can expect from our treatment of the river – that the result should not be terrible?

'You can't have an understanding based on one trip to the river,' the ecologist had told us earlier. 'You have to walk the river at higher flows as well, otherwise you don't know what it's capable of. And we'll traverse this section again at an even lower flow.'

The ecologist and I walk together for a while, splashing across the ripples. He tells me about his trip to the Ahuriri.

'What a beautiful river,' he says. 'It's the only one in that district that's relatively unmodified. The Ahuriri runs from the mountains through Crown land. It's a river in its wild natural state. Oh, and the Ōtemātātā. That's a beautiful river too.'

No-one today is saying the Manuherekia is beautiful.

Once threatened by hydro-electric power schemes, the Ahuriri was protected in 1990 by a national water conservation order on the grounds of its wild and scenic beauty and the biological species it supported. The protection was awarded not only for the main stem of the Ahuriri but also for its tributaries and associated lagoons, ponds, tarns and swamps, from its sources to Lake Benmore.

'What do you think of this?' Brian asks me as we walk a long stretch of stones beside the Manuherekia.

'I feel like crying,' I say. 'I thought the river would always be a source of wonder.'

There's a roaring sound over by the bank as if the river is churning to life again. I turn my head to check, but it's the wind tossing and filtering through the willows. Above us, terns cry out and circle in the sky.

Matt's camera battery is flat. 'Take a picture of the rope swing and the dam,' he tells me. A rope swing dangles abandoned over a pool that is cut off from the river, the water fetid and murky. Nearby, a small dam has been built with stones. Perhaps it created a pool for a child, but now the dam is a ridge of stones on a dry riverbed, evidence that families played here once.

A flood has tossed a pile of willow sticks onto the bank. Christine and I stop to examine them. She picks up a narrow pole.

'That's a good walking stick,' I say. She hands it to me.

'No, you have it,' I say, but she passes me the stick, and it is a help for the following hours of the walk. And there, at last, our vehicles waiting on the edge of the bank. Beyond us, the water flows on towards Alexandra.

The council asks us: 'What sort of river do you want?'

The scientists say: 'We can give you figures and scenarios. We can tell you that at this flow the river will look like this. But it's all up to you, what you as a community choose, what the river will look like.'

The council sends out an invitation: 'Let us know what is important to you – economic survival, cultural values, fishing …'

… always the river is subject to our gaze and to our requirements. Nobody is asking the river what it desires.

'If a river wants to braid, let it braid,' the ecologist said on one of the stretches we walked. 'Don't just confine it to one channel.'

What if a river wants to sing?

What if a river wants to be clean?

What if a river wants nothing between itself and the stones?

What if a river wants to feel each thriving entry of the tributary streams?

What if a river wants to flow along its whole length and not be drained into pools and dry gravel?

What if a river doesn't want to be dammed?

What if a river doesn't want to be 'dewatered'?

What if the council thought about what the river needed in order to thrive, and didn't ask us, the people? For we cannot be trusted. Will enough people who care for the river for the river's sake answer the questions? Or will the questions be answered mainly by those who have a financial stake in the river? They may want a river that only moves enough to bring the water to their gate. Ecologist Mike Joy points out that while community consensus sounds great, it requires compromise from all sides, and therein lies the flaw: 'The reality is that farmers can compromise, industrial and recreational users can compromise, but already stressed freshwater ecosystems cannot.'

But if you go again and again to the waters, there – under the wheeling of skylark, under the wings of blue heron, under the brightness of duck wing, in the shallows where small fish dart, under the willows where the pool is deep and lucid, around the next bend where the light falls so hard on the ripples it splinters and bounces like rain – there you might find your answers.

It is autumn when I come to the last stretch of the river. What had been summer and long hot days on the stones, the pools beckoning under the willows, has turned to frost in the mornings. Late-ripening tomatoes caught frozen on their browned and ruined stalks, and the foggy grass bent with the weight of ice that looks silver in the early morning light.

Along the Manuherekia from Shaky Bridge to the confluence with the Clutha/Mata-Au, the willows are green and yellow and the poplars spires of gold. The sky is deep blue and flawless, no wind to stir the trees or the water so that the river is as burnished as a lake.

Although I am in the bounds of the town, for a while there is no sign of houses or vehicles or people or animals, just the river. Birds chitter in the trees and far off a dog barks, but for some minutes the river is a realm of autumn solitude. I walk on the stones as far as I can until the river turns, and then I take my shoes and socks off and push up my jeans. The water is chilled with the memory of frost and the early snow on the Hawkduns. It's 200 metres now to the confluence. The great river Clutha/Mata-Au flows below Bridge Hill, where houses are colourful in the afternoon light. There are ducks under the willow branches, in small groups on the gravel and flying low over the water.

I walk towards the mouth of the Manuherekia, one foot after the other in the shallow edge of the river. Beside me, the water deepens. There is so much silt from last week's heavy rain, packed between the stones I walk on, each footfall cushioned by mud. The river is deep, quiet, mysterious. It holds the soil washed down from the tributaries and from the fields newly ploughed for winter brassica crops. It holds whatever has been put on that soil.

Yet here, in the still autumn air, the river is beautiful. It is the light that sings over it. The water like a gracious queen, holding wounds deep within yet moving regally, head high, elegant and gracious and alone. From its bright promise as a silver tumbling thread, through tussock under a sky that only saw hill and hawk and rock, to this: aged and slow and laden.

In this stillness the two rivers merge, the Manuherekia moving towards the Clutha/Mata-Au, the Clutha/Mata-Au moving into the Manuherekia. The ducks honk. The water around my feet deepens until I cannot take another step without plunging into the depths. The river is gone from me now, dispersed drop by drop into the stronger current.

I remember how, in only my skin, I lay down in the Ida Burn, in that cool mountain tributary up near the source, filling all the space between stone and the water's surface as if I too were a tributary, or as if the water flowing over me also flowed through me, making us one.

Map for the heart

On the riverbank a tent, possibly abandoned, a shopping trolley on its side, beer bottles, cardboard boxes, damp flags of clothing. The impulse to come to the riverbank perhaps had its home in beauty. The rubbish a symptom of a deeper problem of despoliation and disrespect.

A clattering on the stairs, 6.30 in the morning and three children calling out 'Grandma!' My pen races to write down words about the river, and then they are beside me.

'Did you write all those words?' asks Sonny, who is five. 'How can you write so fast? Are you going to write to the end of the page?'

I tell them I'm writing about my river.

'Does the river flow into a bigger river?' asks Sonny.

'Yes, my river, the Manuherekia, flows into the Clutha/Mata-Au. Just like the Kawarau flows into the Clutha.'

'That's not the Kawarau out by us,' says Phoenix, who is eight. 'That's the Shotover River. That flows into the Kawarau.'

'And the Kawarau flows into the Clutha/Mata-Au. Our rivers are together.'

Lucia, who is three, keeps her hand on my writing book.

'I hold it here, and your hand holds it there,' she says.

'I wrote one page and then another page at school yesterday,' says Phoenix.

They are warm beside me, their favourite soft toys as well – Panda, Teddy, Baby. Outside, the sky is layered blue, mist, the pink striations of dawn. The image of the Manuherekia recedes. It's flowing, mixed up with the Kawarau and their Shotover, all moving towards the ocean.

'Why are you writing about the river?' Phoenix asks.

'Because I care about it,' I say.

And then I want nothing but their tousled heads, and to hold them.

The day Brian and I biked and walked the east branch of the Manuherekia, the radio had forecast southerlies and rain. We travelled through fields of lucerne and irrigated pasture, then tussock and native grass, matagouri, Spaniard grass and the fine-leafed grey shrubs, olearia, *Coprosma propinqua* or mingimingi. And then we were near the confluence of the east and west branches.

I took my camera and ran through grass along a sheep track until I came to where the east clattered into the west. The waters were clear and fast, running musically, eternally, over the stones. Oh Manuherekia, who would transform downstream. I knew your story, but here I was reminded of hope again. There were the hills coming down to the tussocked flats, all gold, the sky grey, the water and rocks grey, the moody wildness and colour of the high country.

We wheeled our bikes into the water of the west branch, which was cool to the knees, the substrate bouldery, and pushed through to the gravel road that climbed ahead to the mountains, the wind in our faces. No farmed animals, no cultivation, no fences or buildings, only the track, the hills and the sound of the river, which up here was the size of a strong alpine stream. We came upon the stream again and again – here wide and braided in a bouldered valley and, higher up, falling over small precipices of rocks, so that even from far above we could hear its rushy, tripletty call. Sun flashed on small glimpses of stream hidden by tussock. Every flank of hill had a crevasse where water ran down, and through matagouri, wetlands, grasses and bunchy snow tussock, these trickles found the stream and the stream gurgled, deepened, ran away down the valley. We were on rewind from the river, the path so steep and rocky we pushed our bikes for kilometres into the hills. Brian's blue cycling jacket was the brightest colour in the damp land, where first there was wind, then rain. I pushed, riding on the flatter stretches, wheels skidding, heart thumping. A hawk with large dark wings flew low above us, swept over the tussock and up into the air.

Around each corner, I thought, surely: the summit will be here. But the track kept rising and twisting, the hills pressing closer until the valley became a channel for tussock and the stream, which we heard but could no longer see. I pushed my bike until I couldn't then placed it on the ground and lay face down on the alpine grass. Brian bent over me.

'I'm all right, I'm all right,' I said. After a minute, the lure of the next corner enticed me up to push the bike again. Around the next corner, another cyclist. He'd biked, he said, from the Ōmarama side of the pass.

'How far to the top of the pass?' I asked. He looked at his recorder.

'Seven kilometres.'

On we pushed. A golden hill rose in front of us. Surely that would be the pass. Then around a corner Brian called out his tyre was flat and the pump wasn't working.

'You carry on a bit,' he said. 'I'll try and sort it out.'

Map for the heart

I laid my bike in the gravel and kept walking. Below, the rushy stream gurgled and poured. The air chilled with a smell of wet grass and rock. Around the next corner the track veered sharp left and climbed steeply to the pass to the Mackenzie country. If the clouds had cleared I might have seen Aoraki, Cloud-piercer. Instead, my eyes and my heart followed the stream, under the track and upwards to where the golden hills came together. Beyond them was only sky. There, in silver threads, the Manuherekia begins, up there in the silence and the rain.

For weeks after walking the river I felt unsettled. I longed to be back in the water, just walking, with every corner ahead of me a delight. Constrained in the car crossing a bridge, the river below, I felt like a prisoner looking out on a freedom I'd once had. If it rained I wanted to feel the strength in the river's flow; if it was windy, to hear the willows' surge, loud as a long-gone train, and see the leaves tumbling to the water.

The river had been my refuge, I realised, my peacemaker, head-healer, teacher. Waking early each day to tug on wet boots and warm tights before driving to the river to find a way down the bank. In those seven days there was no other reason in life except to see where the water led me.

But if my days on land are charged by loss of the river, so is my attitude to society. Whereas before I had sat for long hours in the Environment Court hearings for the Lindis River, listening to those who stood for the water users, interested but alarmed, now I feel despair and distaste. What was happening in the fight for the rights to the Lindis would also happen for the Manuherekia.

In its natural state the Manuherekia is about a four-cumec river. In summer, water users take the river down to 0.8 or 0.9 of a cumec. The National Institute of Water and Atmospheric Research estimates the natural flow in the lower reaches is about a quarter of what it would be without irrigation takes. The water users will petition to be allowed to continue to take three quarters of a river's strength. I see it in the letters to the newspaper and around the table with the council. For some, the cost of their pivot irrigators means that if they can't continue to take all they need, their enterprise will no longer be viable.

What does it mean for the river when it barely clears a depth above our ankles, silt covers its stones and long threads of algae sag in its waters, when mayflies don't hatch and the small living beings and sleek eels are no longer able to live in it?

Thirty years ago a date was set for the re-allocation of water rights on the Manuherekia. Every water user knows this. The date was set to decide a safer minimum flow for the river and its biotic community. But what is this level? Why not say half the water for the river, half for the water users? A technical report by Otago Regional Council in 2017 recommends just that: a flow of 2–3 cumecs at Ophir. But the emails coming to me from contractors and lawyers representing water users show they will use whatever data they can to prove: we can take this much before the river is ruined. I don't even want to read them.

How close they want to go.

And I am sick of the fight already. Before we even go to court. Before we even go to mediation. Before we even listen to the final summing up.

The river is strong enough to wear its way down through schist. It is long enough to link a high mountain valley with the great Clutha/Mata-Au. It stretches between those two homes, vulnerable and individual, at the beck and call of the powers of wind and rain and snowmelt, and utterly harnessed to human desire. It is a cattle beast on a truck, hemmed in, on the way to slaughter, eyes rolling, fear a stench on the breeze. It is something we want to consume.

I am changed by the river. When the time comes I will get up again and speak. I'm speaking now. But I have seen how humans stand apart from the natural world and say: this is not us but *for* us. To say the river has rights and needs, to say the river deserves our responsibility to further generations, to say the river is one being from mountain torrent to the wide, luminous stretch between shingled banks, is to go against those who have the voice of power, against those who say we need 'the courage to dam the rivers'. I have lost my faith in those with power. What will happen to our rivers? To *the* rivers, not *our* rivers. What will happen to the Manuherekia?

Can we lie down on the river's banks among the slime and silt? Can we glue ourselves to pivot irrigators? Can we stand on the riverbanks with signs? Or shall we walk the river? Yes, each one who would use it, who desires its strength and bounty, must walk its length. Not just gaze upon it; not say, without knowledge, 'This is not a terrible river.' Know the river. Be with it along its whole length.

Mayors – do this.

Councillors – do this.

Scientists – do this.

All those who love to look upon a river – do this.

Young people – do this, so you will know what is being drained from your future.

American agrarian Wendell Berry writes:

> We have the world to live in on the condition that we will take good care of it. And take good care of it, we have to know it. And to know it and to be willing to take care of it, we have to love it.

In his essay 'Land Ethic', American writer Aldo Leopold says: 'A thing is right when it tends to preserve the integrity, stability, and beauty of the biotic community; it is wrong when it tends otherwise.'

Mike Joy says: 'Healthy functioning ecosystems are no longer just a "nice to have", they are a prerequisite for the continuation of civilization, not to speak of our responsibility to future generations.'

The river says …

> (you know what the river is saying
> without being told. You hear
> what the river is singing
> without knowing the words
> to the song.
>
> –Brian Turner)

Under autumn sky, in a pool deep from snowmelt and rain, the surface so bright and pure it holds sky and golden poplar and sun and duck on its surface, a mirror reflecting this world we've been bequeathed. And in the air the coolness of frost soon to descend, the whiff of snow from where the river begins, that age-old cycle the river holds in its sheen, in its mystery. Willow leaves, small golden offerings, on its skin.

Blackstone Hill

No man coming here need fear but that he can do something ...

Otago Daily Times, *1864*

BLACKSTONE HILL is a shadowy hulk beyond my vegetable garden this morning. The low hills are lit with the morning sun, the willows lime-green, the broom bursting out with yellow. I've said to Barry, the neighbouring farmer who has helped me with grazing, 'No more cattle on my paddocks, I want to plant the wetlands with natives.' There's a small kōwhai forest already started in one broom group, firewood trees in another, both lots only a foot high but sheltered.

Still, I am no grazier, I don't seek to use animals anymore, and so the grass has grown lank with spring growth, especially with this rain one day on, one day off, and temperatures reaching to thirty degrees in between. Though yesterday, frost.

I told Barry at the pub, 'My potato leaves have burned off.'

'Didn't you hear the news say there'd be a one-degree frost? Didn't you go out and cover them?'

'No.' I struggle to find a reason. 'Too lazy,' I say, and Barry laughs.

'I haven't planted mine yet,' he says.

Not lazy for work, but too slow to make connections again after the winter: that this land stings. And too protected by a supermarket in Alexandra forty minutes' drive away down the valley, or the historic General Store six doors down the footpath.

I think of the waves of people who have come through here forming colonies of one kind or another. First came the flint gatherers, toolmakers and moa hunters. Next came the runholders, referred to as New Zealand's 'rural elite' on account of having won vast tracts of land in ballots, taking in the Hawkdun mountains, Rough Ridge, Blackstone Hill and the valley floors. The goldminers came like a swarm into the gullies and folds of the land, followed by storekeepers, hoteliers, butchers, bakers, blacksmiths and domestics. Racemen diverted water for the miners. Settlers followed, taking up small leases of land, then the railwaymen with their wheelbarrows and shovels, bringing the line from Dunedin through here on the way to Cromwell. What was once the Cobb and Co. stables and coaching stop in our main street has morphed into Beckers Transport. There are truck drivers in the village, and writers, and others who have come here – not for industriousness or to win some richness from the land but for quiet, for the one short road that leads out of town, for the light on the ranges and the days when little is heard but the birds or, for local colour, the sound of Barry mustering with his dogs on Rough Ridge.

Once I begin reading history, the land around me becomes something other: the folds of Rough Ridge now the place where miners once walked carrying their blankets, their pans, their small sack of victuals, maybe even across my own boggy land, oxen floundering, the packies scarlet with their language. And on that other hill, Blackstone, hundreds of miners in their tents in the cold gullies and the sweltering heat.

But first, around seven hundred years ago, Waitaha, Kāti Māmoe and then Kāi Tahu iwi camped here in their own versions of tents, circular summer huts of raupō and tussock.

'Barry's father Bill always said there were three Māori ovens behind where my hayshed is now,' neighbouring farmer Trevor Beck told me. 'Poke around if you wish.'

In the long grass I find nothing but a golden sarsen stone, maybe 400mm long, the size of a large mudbrick. Sarsen, or silcrete, once named 'Chinaman' by the early goldminers, is an extremely hard silica-cemented quartz-rich sandstone. The mostly smooth boulders are sometimes covered in yellow-brown rusty iron oxide. Farmer Robert Gardyne tells me there's many a farm implement been broken on a sarsen stone. I once came across glistening boulders of it in a wondrous stretch of the Ida Burn stream. Under water they shine in the light like gold.

On Trevor and Judy's farm, Triplet Creek, where the Ida Burn, Gorge Creek and Hills Creek come together, early Māori brought silcrete down from Rough Ridge to flake for tools, mostly for hunting and preparing moa.

'When I ploughed my field years ago,' Trevor told me, 'I found a sack-load of flints and gave it to Otago Museum.' He describes one: pink and white and gold and grey, big enough for a large hand, two sides flaked to a sharp edge. I can see the silcrete quarry from my dining room window as I look up at Rough Ridge, the slopes flecked with the pale of stone and nature taking over: broom, matagouri, rosehip, a solitary pine.

Two springs ago after a big flood, visiting children pottering around by the stream at Trevor and Judy's saw something pink in the flood-torn bank. Their son Andrew recognised it straight away – a conch shell, taonga puoro, a musical instrument. Otago Museum verified it as one of three, and the largest, found in Otago.

'They don't often last in an archaeological site,' a representative from the museum told me, 'so it was exciting for one to be found in good condition.' The taonga puoro, from the Pacific Islands and possibly over 700 years old, now belongs to the Crown. The museum will act as custodian until the shell's final resting place is decided.

These waves of people came with treasures and skills from their homelands: from the South Pacific and Europe, from China and the British Isles. Further up Hills Creek on the site of the early township, below the slopes of Blackstone Hill, are the remains of the last of the eleven hotels that once stood there (the Carrier's Arms, the Montezuma, the Ulster ...). The Prince Alfred is now a heap of corrugated iron, weathered beams and planks under a hawthorn tree. There's a doorway still standing. I walk through it and see a fireplace of corrugated iron, and when I bend to peer inside, rows of weathered mudbricks lining the sides.

Mount Ida Chronicle, 28 February 1878

On Friday evening, 22nd, Blackstone Hill mustered its residents in right good style to receive and welcome the Rev. James McCosh Smith. A very excellent tea was provided by Mr and Mrs Inder, of the Prince Alfred Hotel, the tables being plentifully furnished with cake, buns, sandwiches, and all kinds of fresh fruit ... The Rev. McCosh Smith gave an able address, basing his remarks upon the happiness of work and illustrating his subject with experiences he had met with at home. Mrs Anderson sang very sweetly during the evening. Mr Johnstone and Mr Ash also sang songs which pleased everyone. Mr de Lautour, being called upon, also spoke a few words in favour of 'hero worship' and expressing his pleasure at meeting Blackstone Hill on a less serious occasion than a political meeting. During the evening a number of hymns of rare beauty and pathos were selected by the Chairman, who himself presided at the harmonium all the night. Being called upon for a song from himself he gave 'The Land o' the Leal' very nicely.

The track

Not far up the farm track on Robert and Rosemary Gardyne's farm on the slopes of Blackstone Hill, fellow tramper Graeme Male and I come across an artful, natural arrangement on the dirt – a lamb's tail with tight wool covering and next to it an oval egg, possibly that of a duck. Why a duck laid an egg there on the track next to the tail is a mystery, and a reminder, on this day with a new ridge to explore, of how little I know of the world of creatures and land.

These hills are quiet. There is the sound of my boots landing on the dirt and lifting off, Graeme's boots likewise, and the water in my bottle sloshing. There are no sheep calling, nor even birds. No tractor moves. The road far below. After last night's rain the earth is warm and damp.

On a corner against a bank there's a conglomeration of manure where sheep have gathered and slept. They choose this elevated site instinctively, Robert tells me later, because from here they can see any danger approaching. This morning the night's manure is made fresh again by the damp and the smell is bitter and dark. There are odours, too, of decomposing grass and fresh growing grass, a fecund land smell. Graeme and I take the track to the left through Spaniard grass and tough red tussock with its less flexible fronds, sharp like toetoe, and the graceful, billowy and softer silver tussock.

A wire fence curves like wings around the edge of a cliff where tussock clings to schist and sometimes white quartz. Matagouri. A stream running clear with sky. And everywhere there is green – greener, says Graeme, than he's ever seen it. It's his fourth trip on foot to the peak.

This side of Blackstone Hill lies to the east and is shaded from the baking afternoon sun. Later we'll see the contrast on the ridge, where paddocks laying to the west are brown and dry as if they've been obliterated by chemical spray. On this more benign slope, grass prospers and so do the lambs. Robert told me of his preference for leaving tussock on a farm, because at this altitude it gathers moisture for the grass each night and gives shelter to the soil from the wind and sun.

We climb higher, the track turning and turning. I only have to keep my feet lifting and placing, while all about is blue sky – so different from yesterday's walk up Rocks Creek into a head wind under a grey sky. I tell Graeme about the creek flowing off Mt St Bathans, how astounding to see it flowing steeply downhill. 'I'm a lowlander,' I say. 'The stream behind my home runs along what seems like a flat plane. I thought that's what streams did. Not that headlong rush downwards.'

'Gravity is the parent of all nature,' Graeme says. 'Everything is in a state of falling: the rocks rolling down, water seeping down, rain ...'

Here, though, there is evidence of a time when everything lifted. We pass by rocky tors taller than trees, larger than houses, uplifted slab upon slab out of the earth and all facing northeast. The rocks were forced out of the ground by earthquake faults. 'You can't even begin to imagine the force required to shift them,' Robert said to me. His neighbour had a rock topple down the slope onto a fence. There was nothing for it but to build a new fence line around it.

The further, bigger ranges – the Hawkduns in front of us, Mt St Bathans to the left and the Kakanuis to the right – are northwest-trending mountains, uplifted 5 million years ago from a base of greywacke. The hill beneath us, the Dunstans to the left, Rough Ridge and the far Rock and Pillars are all northeast-trending block hills, folded upwards 3 million years ago from a base of schist.

We tramp up onto the ridgeline, into a field of tussock, the great tors around us. One, a triangular rock roughly twenty metres high, was filmed for Peter Jackson's movie *The Hobbit*. In this very pasture were hobbits with long feet and ears, the production crew, the black cameras, the call for silence on set ...

Graeme and I wend our way through the land. No sheep, no other people, no farm workers or miners or film crews. No birds. It is a land of rocks and sky and quiet.

Burdock and fleece

'Burdock, briar rose, horehound, thistles, barley grass, all devaluing the fleece wool,' Robert says. 'Not to mention twitch, redshank, gorse and broom. Ferrets, stoats, rabbits, wild pigs, blowflies, lice – if we didn't have all that it would be heaven up here,' he says. 'And there are the insect pests: springtail, nysius, clover root weevil, porina, Argentine stem weevil, aphids. Except for the native moth porina, all the other weeds, pests and predators were introduced. We really did mess this country up, and now we're left to deal with it as best we can.'

Robert's in wet-weather gear and I'm in shorts, the wind relentless and icy. It's the weaning muster. Below us, the village arranged along the road. My own house, red-roofed, hunkered down. The townie.

Robert points out to me the plantain, and blue-flowered chicory growing around the pond. 'I've sown the paddocks with plantain and chicory. Herbs,' he explains, 'for all the minerals. I suspect most farmers give more thought to what their sheep eat than most people do to their own diets.'

Clover green around the base of the tussocks. Coprosma, the divaricating persistent shrubs, toetoe buoyant in the gullies.

'Go up to the gate and wait there,' he says. The wind is strong out of the south. I crouch in front of a tussock, lean into its almost-warmth. The tussocks on the hillside ripple and thrash. The other musterers, his son and daughter and neighbouring friends, are out of sight, spread over the flanks of the hill. In this wind I can't even hear them shouting. I stand up, searching the tawny grasses. Robert appears beside me with directions.

'Go seventy metres down that ridge,' he says. 'Go sideways into the matagouri on the north side of the ridge and make a big noise; come back, go seventy metres, then sideways back into the matagouri and make a big noise. Keep doing that all the way along the ridge. Go down to that rock and wait till you see me.'

I slip sideways on the slope, yell again and again. No sheep. Only rocks and the rocky tors.

'Heyaaa!' I yell into the matagouri, and a ewe and a lamb with a long tail, one missed in the tailing muster, erupt from the thorny shrubs and bound downhill. They leap past the farmer. I slither the last metres to rock.

'Good work finding those two,' Robert says.

Wind, then slanting rain, then brief sun. Enough sun that the tussocks shine and the sheep below us in their rumbling mob are golden.

Golden days

Otago Daily Times, 24 October 1864

The diggings at Blackstone Hill … have created considerable excitement lately among both the mining and business communities … Blackstone Hill is a continuation of the Ragged Ridge, and forms its northern extremity but presents by no means any remarkable feature that would cause special attention to be directed towards it. The diggings, better known as Hills Creek, are on the east face of the range. Mr Hill, who keeps a store in the township, lays claim to having made the discovery, but a digger named Wilson, having for a mate a German, known under the soubriquet of Groggy, disputed the honers [sic] with him; still, as the diggings have been found out, it matters little at present by whom.

It is a distant 43 miles E.N.E. from the Dunstan, 7 miles from the Dunstan Creek, 15 from Hogburn, 28 from Hamiltons, and about 110 from Dunedin. The township is situated on the flat of the Ida Burn Valley and has a running creek passing nearly in its midst. It comprises some fifty business places; among which are eleven hotels, three butchers and three bakers, the rest being made up of storekeepers and other traders.

The tops

On the peak of Blackstone Hill there's a trigonometrical station. Graeme and I climb up the slabs of rock and wedge ourselves in among the smaller boulders to eat and drink. I have bananas and cherries; Graeme has a bag of nuts and a health bar. He passes me a chunk and I pass him the bag of cherries. There are still hours to go: three hours to reach this spot, another three along the ridge, and then an hour down. I question Graeme on his procedures for mountain tramps.

Water? He carries two litres in a camel pack. I have one litre in my bottle.

Food for a longer trip? Porridge.

'Like the gold miners,' I say. 'They carried a bag of oats and a billy.'

'I'll take a cooked dinner for the first night,' Graeme says, 'and dehydrated meals for the next nights. For drink, I take hot chocolate.' For a moment I imagine how it would feel to sit on a slope alone, boiling up water for a rich sweet drink, contemplating the terrain below, the coolness of sky.

We buckle on our gaiters and climb backwards down the rocks ('face inwards on the rocks, not outwards,' Graeme says) and keep walking north. Through the barbed-wire fence on the next property hieracium has colonised broad sweeps at the foot of the rocks, the land like tundra, hard and dry. The flat blue-green leaves of this weed allow nothing else to grow and it has prospered here, as elsewhere in the dry Central Otago climate. On the Gardynes' side we move through the richness of matagouri, Spaniard grass, tussock, our calves protected by the gaiters.

I had imagined a ridgeline like a razorback, like the two-dimensional image of the tops I saw from below, a sharp outline with rocky tors. But up here the land is wide, carved into successive bowls so that we walk through rooms of tussock edged by slopes of hill and rock. We can no longer see the far valley, only the tops of ranges: Rough Ridge to the right, the Hawkduns to the front, the top of Mt St Bathans and the Dunstans to the left. In warm air we move alone through the curved land, each bowl with its own ramparts of tors, and here a swamp that spreads out, its green rushes to be skirted. A paradise duck flings up out of the reeds and flies honking above us.

'The best advice I've received about tramping,' Graeme says, 'was from my snowcraft instructor, Jaz Morris in the Alpine Club, and he learnt it from his mountaineer teacher. The three things of utmost importance – surefootedness, balance and rhythm.'

Otago Daily Times, 24 October, 1864

The principal diggings are at the Four-mile or Woolshed, so named for their being in the close vicinity of a building there, owned by the Messrs Shields on whose run the diggings are situated ... The workings are on the spurs of two hills and in the gullies between ... The ground is either wrought by puddling, or by sinking a shaft and driving ... Most of the nuggets are highly crystalline, and contain quartz, and have evidently not travelled far from their matrix.

The population may be estimated as follows: Woolshed, or Four-mile, 400; Peg-leg Gully, 50; German Gully, 60. Working on patches in the ranges, 220; Blue gully, 12; Round tent, 20; Hatters, 12; Simon's, 6; Old Man, 20; in the Township, 150; making a total of 848 persons. About a fortnight since the population was half as much again, but they have left for other places.

Spur

Instead of following the ridgeline till it flattens out at the highway, Graeme and I take a tongue of land that leads away from the crest. We descend through ryegrass and native grass interspersed with tussock. These gentler lower slopes are more recognisable as farmland than wild lands. The rocky tors are more like cut-off chimneys than the megalithic stones of the ridgeline. We walk past an old orchard of apple trees, and hawthorn sheathed in white blossom. To rest the bunched muscles in my legs, I stand still for a moment on the grass and look up. The sky has a depth of blue more akin to a winter's day. One set of towering white cloud over far Mt St Bathans. A hawk gliding on a rising thermal, its passing arrowed wings a brief flicker of shade.

We are near the gullies where once there were thriving mining camps, the sites of Woolshed Diggings and German Gully. This close, and nothing to show that people lived and hoped here. But then, unexpectedly, among the long grass and beneath curtains of muehlenbeckia, the remnants of stonework from what might have been a dam the miners constructed 155 years ago to store water.

Otago Witness, 25 February 1865

Since my last, nothing much of importance has transpired here, if I except the completion of the two races to German Gully … perhaps the finest work of the kind in the province … It commences at the foot of the Hawkdun Ranges, and after running some twenty miles, it reaches the workings immediately above the township. From thence to German Gully is a distance of about three miles, and in this length a work of great magnitude and expense has just been completed.

The land here offered much to the miner and the settler. Forget the cold and the heat; there was water from the mountains, and soil, as the *Otago Witness* reported in 1864:

… almost everywhere possesses great agricultural capabilities, and is a fine black loam, having a clay subsoil, and doubtless, when brought into cultivation, will produce very fine crops.

The miner J.H. Watmuff, or Bendigo Jack as he was known, had his own opinion of the land here:

> I never saw a stick growing that would make a pen holder – the country to this point bearing one uniform character, barren and desolate and ever will be, the ground being too hilly and rocky for cultivation, and too cold and bleak for pastoral purposes except in summertime.

But there was coal in these hills according to the *Otago Witness* in 1864:

> Lignite is everywhere abundant and of extremely good quality ... within a quarter of a mile of the township, a bed of this valuable fuel can be traced for upwards of a mile and within but a few feet of the surface ... the charge is eight shillings for a single horse load, ten shillings for a larger.

The lignite is still in the land here, in names (Coalpit Road) and in the seams sometimes exposed by water. One morning after the flooded Ida Burn had receded, I found many deposits of black coal on the scoured-out paddock where almost a thousand square metres of grass and broom had been stripped back to stone. It looked as if, overnight, the miners of old had descended unseen onto the riverbank and built campfires on the stones, leaving their heaped and cold black ash in triangular piles.

In German Gully, at Woolshed Diggings and the other sites, this lignite, delivered by horse to the campsites, cooked mutton, damper and oats. It kept the miners warm when mist descended. Even in summer sleet could brush against the tussock and the horses' warm flanks, or snow lie on the ground fifteen centimetres deep and more in the gullies.

When the easily won gold ran out, the miners looked to settle in the valley that had become their home. In her book about Blackstone Hill cemetery, historian Judy Beck cites Janet Cowan: 'On July 9 1869, an area of 2500 acres [1000ha] of agricultural land on Blackstone Hill Run was set apart for occupation and there were many applications for the leases in the 1870s.'

In 1879 Elizabeth and William Agnew took up the lease of a section at Blackstone Hill and built a small earthen house there. Judy relates their story. When the Agnews couldn't pay their lease, the land was sold out from under them at auction:

> The moment that the auctioneer brought down his hammer and declared it sold, Agnew and his wife rushed like furies at the cottage which was a frail

building with mud walls, and literally tore and kicked it in pieces crying, 'You'll never get our house!'

They were a quaint couple, the man with no waistcoat, a grey flannel shirt which hung out all round his waist, the woman wearing a crinoline and dress which had perhaps been her mother's wedding costume forty years before, and waving a huge umbrella of the size and style beloved by Mrs Gamp. The woman would stand waving her umbrella while she volubly held forth on her rights and the man would hop around closing his fists and making audible threats.

The couple sued the auctioneer, harassed their lawyer and even travelled to Wellington to beleaguer Prime Minister Sir Harry Atkinson and other ministers for compensation, but to no avail. For many years all they were left to live in was a dilapidated tent. 'The couple ended their years in destitution,' Judy records, 'but the storekeepers in the area took turns supplying their needs free of charge.'

The rounds

'Last year when I was chasing cattle out of the broom by the Ida Burn,' Trevor Beck tells me, 'I came across three rounded raised shapes. They look like they were for something – perhaps the goldminers had a hut there, or early Māori. It makes sense, they're by the stream and near where the middens were.'

I try looking for the circles myself with his directions, crouching through broom that tangles above my head. And there they are, three round raised soil areas growing only grass, so that among the broom they are like fairy circles. On one is a hand-sized piece of greywacke, chipped to a sharp edge. Or are the notions of history getting to me? Seven hundred years is a long time for silt and flooding to take its toll, to do its own shaping and creating.

I send photos of the rounds to archaeologist Matthew Sole.

'Pretty sure these are likely to be old mud/sod huts', he replies. 'Along with the early Māori evidence, there are numerous sites of mining, ground working and sluicing visible when you review early aerials and survey plans. There is a record of an early archaeological site for tool flakes and middens

in the vicinity of Trevor Becks' place.' He attaches the paperwork, written up
in 1967, and we arrange a site visit. For now, the rounds remain a mystery.
Matt has said not to disturb them in any way.

Knowing, as I walk around, that history surrounds me, I begin to
understand how fleetingly we are upon the earth, and how grinding and
inexorable and elemental is the land we live upon. It was submerged and
uplifted, it gave up its gold and its mountain grasses, it submits to whatever
we do upon its flanks, and by and by we are cast away. We live where the
Agnews, or others like them, howled for vengeance and justice, their flimsy
tent crackling with frost and wind. Here in these gullies Henry Armitage
dug himself a cave to live in while he mined for gold, and roofed it with tin.
Later, with a wife and eventually nine children, he built a sod house, which
too has melted away. A house built of mudbricks – made of trampled earth
and tussock by his sons George and Jim with their draft horse – still stands,
and will outlast even its present owners as it outlasted Henry and those who
came after him.

We live as if there is no past or future; no time when we didn't walk upon
the land and no time when our breath won't be here or even remembered.
The former people of Blackstone Hill emerge as stories from long ago but
not connected to us. What do they tell us, if not that everything passes?
They died flung from wagons and drowned in coalpits; of childbirth,
dehydration, undiagnosed pneumonia and foul play; lonely on hillsides, in
gaol or in their rooms, destitute or the owners of all that surrounded them.
I don't know what the gift of their stories can be unless it is to deepen my
knowledge: to cycle past the reserve near Hills Creek and know this was a
township; to know that in the broom there by the Ida Burn are remnants of
the existence of early people, their lives rich, too, with the clarity of stream,
of sunsets blazing over Blackstone Hill, of the unexpected brilliance of
snow on the ranges and the light golden on tussock, the way tussock flows
like water in the wind. What does it matter that broom now grows tangled
over the place where once they lived? We whizz past, our pedals turning.
The sweet pea-smell of the broom flowers, the bright deep blue of the sky.
Perhaps it always and only ever comes to this: exhilaration. One way or
another, as fleeting, as dependable and beautiful as the frost or the moon, a
crescent hanging in a turquoise sky.

Reflections

In Oregon in the Cascade mountains there's a 6400-hectare forest known as the H.J. Andrews Experimental Forest. Since 1948 this watershed for Lookout Creek has been dedicated to the quest for knowledge rather than timber. Into its gullies and streams, within its 'dim deepwood of massive and mossbound trees', have come ecologists, biologists, botanists, and geomorphologists with equipment, notes and technology. And since 2003, writers too have come as part of the Long-Term Ecological Reflections programme. They come 'to walk, observe, reflect and record their insights,' writes Charles Goodrich, one of the editors of *Forest Under Story*, which records the scientists' and writers' 'inquiry into ecological and human change spanning generations'. What does it help us to understand, to walk beneath Douglas firs 700–800 years old, among the fallen and rotting deadwood, among the brief evergreen violets and baby hemlocks? Maybe to comprehend that our world's history is one of the 'disintegration and reassembly of ecosystems'.

Brian Turner travelled and stayed at the forest as invited poet in 2011. He wrote:

> ... nobody
> knows how much time we have
> to piece it all together either
>
>   nor how many mistakes we can make
> and survive.

The Reflections programme is intended to continue for 200 years. 'The long view,' Goodrich says, 'helps remind us that we can never find a permanent solution or conclusion to any challenge, because the societal context and even the environmental context continually change.' But when people pay close attention to specific places, wherever those are, 'their study of place will reveal broad truths that go beyond place', and this can help us, he says, become 'more attuned to both the presence of the past ... and the seriousness of our responsibility for shaping the future'.

Grass

Early December, and the winds are blustering across the paddock. The long grass ripples and shivers. A flock of birds, large enough to be starlings I think, lifts from the seedy grasses to hover and dip again. Brian leans on my bench.

'I thought I'd better come and tell you,' he says, 'there's some around here not happy about the state of your paddocks. Come summer your place could be a fire risk, they say, and threaten their businesses and homes.'

I look out the window and think of when I first bought my land. The grass was waist high, burnt golden. The acres rippling tawny as if they were tussock again, as if all that once lived here hadn't changed. I was looking forward to that sight again, and the birds wheeling and soaring above the grains, the paddocks becoming their own wild ecosystems: timothy, cocksfoot, ryegrass, Yorkshire fog, buttercup, reeds, clover, skinks, frogs, plovers, and the hundreds of natives I'd already planted in the broom and the wetlands – kōwhai, raupō, cabbage trees and flax.

'But over the years, other summers, when it's been long no-one's said anything,' I venture.

'There are more people living here now,' Brian says. 'There are other pressures.'

In the evening I try three contractors who could mow the land for hay. They are away, or at work. But Barry answers my call.

'Your paddocks are too stony,' he says. 'I wouldn't risk my equipment there. It can be $55,000 for a mower. It's too easy for it to be wrecked at your place.'

'Then what can I do?'

'The only thing is to put stock back in there,' he says. 'And we can try a hot wire around your trees.'

'I didn't think my grass would grow this fast,' I say. I'd been away for weeks, helping look after my mother.

'It was always going to happen,' Barry says.

I am thankful for his help and advice, but when I hang up I begin to cry. Probably because I know that I haven't learnt enough yet, or done enough, to know what I'm doing. But also because, in a village, there are lines that can be drawn. In the country there are people who have generations of knowledge about looking after the land, and others who don't. And I begin to feel self-pity for being alone and overwhelmed at times by all the travel to visit my family; for not wanting to eat animals in a community that grows them; for wanting a wilderness that could mean danger to others; for being offside when I wanted the peace of oneness. Thinking perhaps that peace doesn't happen anywhere, not even in a community as small, as old, as varied as this.

'Every farmer has had to struggle with the land,' Robert tells me later. 'We've all had to come to terms with nature.'

Broom, a brightness of yellow under the willows. Snow on Mt St Bathans. Above Blackstone Hill, a massing of grey clouds but not yet rain. The wind relentless, the grass bending in its path.

Three Paths to Rough Ridge

ROUGH RIDGE is right outside my window. It's what I see when standing at my kitchen sink – the tors, the tors, those dark sentinels on a hill ablaze with afternoon light. It's so near, and climbable: a ten-minute walk through the village, past the General Store and the pub, over the cycle trail and across Barry's paddock to a gate, after which the land rises into wildness and rocks. The action of placing my foot among stones is enough to keep me anchored in the presence of light and texture and smell, of lichen, sheep droppings and thorn. I think it is the always-possibility of the climb that appeals – the fact I live here, *here*, and not in a street where the nearest hill is a car-trip away, if there at all. So much wildness, right at my nose. I bend my head to my computer and work.

But what of those whose work, whose life, is to be out on the slopes, who don't have to make a choice to go 'outdoors', for whom being outdoors is their way of being? Even in a truck cab, sliding on a steep slope, they are aware of the land – its tilt, its gravel or mud, the depth of stream, the height of matagouri.

'I never stop appreciating it,' Robert Gardyne says. 'But the land is always a responsibility to a farmer.'

'Do you think about the weather all the time?' I ask.

'You have to,' he says. 'Everything we do depends on the weather. When you want rain, get up expecting it to be fine. That's how you cope.'

Path one

Like Blackstone Hill, there are dips on Rough Ridge as if a large hand has scooped them out. Here snowmelt and rainwater collect and the hollows are edged with marshes and reeds 600 metres up on a dry windswept hillside. Brian and I had walked from the highway, from the beginning of the slope of Rough Ridge towards two tors that stood like a gateway, guarded by magpies high on the rock. We passed between them, were cawed at. So many tors of otherworldly stature, we turned our heads to gaze as we walked past – rock formations ten, twenty, thirty metres high, dwarfing us.

'Which way now?' Brian asks. 'We could skirt the top and keep going along the side of the hill?' But I want to go to the highest point, and gesture upwards to where the rocks flare along the skyline. We pass beneath the huge wires that bring power from the Clyde dam, not hesitating under them, and clamber through matagouri, past white bones scattered on the slopes and places where sheep camp out, the grass flattened and covered in manure that is heating and pungent in the sun.

We climb the ridge and walk past the huge tor. Brian stops and looks back.

'Are you thinking of climbing it?' I ask him.

'Thinking of it,' he says as he moves towards it. I follow him, and when I see him trying this way and that to get up a steep slope covered in speargrass, I walk around to the other side which presents a rock face, easy enough to begin with until I'm stopped by a section of rock leading straight up. I try getting one boot up on a ledge, test the rock above it for strength. Shift my foot to another ledge which begins to crumble and break away. Brian appears over the top and looks down at me.

'All you need is three points of contact,' he tells me. Two hands, one boot.

'There's nowhere flat to put my boot. I don't know if I can hold myself up there.'

'You haven't got far to fall if you do,' he says. I look behind me. It's not like I'll fall off the side of the mountain. It's two metres at most but onto speargrass, stones, matagouri. 'Here,' Brian reaches a hand down to me. 'Grip my wrist,' and I hold onto him.

Braced like that I commit to the climb, reaching my boot up and Brian taking weight for me. I end up pressed against him, both of us pinned now to the rock face until he can slither sideways and I climb beyond him. We scrabble up the rest of the tor and sit on the top. I look at the cuts on my arm where blood wells and feel as if I've been blooded – not just an amble across paddocks then, but something risky. The two of us working together, trusting, to go up that face.

We eat our lunch there, bananas and nuts and dates and a drink of water.

'How do you think your life in the outdoors has affected you?' I ask Brian.

He looks around at the far hills – Blackstone Hill and the Home Hills, far Mt St Bathans. And always that line of the Hawkdun Range and Mt Ida.

'The way mountaineering has affected me? I think about what to do before I do it,' he says. 'On the mountains, you'd be looking at a slope and thinking what's the best way to climb across it. Whether you need to rope together with your partner in case one of you gets into trouble. And whether to take the longer route that was easier.

'And with sailing,' he says, 'in certain weather and winds you wouldn't go up on the foredeck without a belt to clip onto the rail. And you'd get a hand on the rail before you reached back and unclipped yourself to move.

'So mostly I do think about the way to approach things. I'm not saying I'm a paragon of how I do things, but I take the precautionary principle. In a cycling race I'd think about what was ahead, where the wind would be, what was around the corner. And if it was a corner I didn't know, especially how sharp it would be, I'd back off on speed.'

The precautionary principle, he's often told me, is how we need to be looking at the way the world is going. Back off a bit till we know what's around the corner.

The sky is gauzy with cloud. 'Subdued', Brian calls it, and the photos I take are too, not like the brilliant blue sky of the Blackstone Hill climb. Here it's all a muted colour scheme: the sky, rocks, parched ground, the scattered bones, the grey matagouri, the black magpies, the wingspan of a hawk, the dusty sheep pressed into crevices in the tors for shade and rest.

I'd heard there was a kōwhai on Rough Ridge. Others have sought to find it without luck, and still others must have come across it unexpectedly as we have, clambering down a damp gully and up towards its graceful branches and exuberance of fronds, a marvel in this landscape. There's a kōwhai high on Blackstone Hill too. Robert had noticed it one day from a hillside on their farm, but it took his son and him two years to find the tree in a hidden valley. Where have they come from, these graceful and gnarled trees? Growing against all odds in snow and storm in the coldest and hottest valley in New Zealand. One tree on each range of hills flanking the Ida Valley.

'I've thought about it a lot, how these trees have survived for hundreds of years,' Robert said to me one day. 'And I think it's because they have grown up through rocks. It's enabled them to survive the harsh winters, much colder than what we have now. The sun heats the rocks up during the day and the heat radiates during the night, protecting the trees from frost. And the rocks shade the ground during the hot, hot summers and shelter it from the moisture sucking nor'west winds.'

There are seedpods hanging in clusters on the kōwhai. Emptied, I think, but when I open one there are yellow seeds. I gather a handful of pods to take down. I'll give some to Robert.

Otago Witness, 23 January 1890

Maniototo county has had two bays allotted to it in the [New Zealand and South Seas] exhibition and the committee that was entrusted with the work of obtaining for the court exhibits representative of their district have discharged their duties in a most praiseworthy manner … splendid wheat grown at Eweburn, Sowburn, Hamilton, Kyeburn and Gimmerburn … at Maruimato at an altitude of 1800ft [550m] … sheaves of oats, wheat and barley … rye … The Ida Valley Milling Company are to the fore with beautiful stone-dressed flour … As yet there is no wool on view … The Maniototo is also a mining district of no mean value and the various companies and parties working in it have made a very creditable exhibition of gold.

The exhibition also included washdirt, coal, lignite, scheelite, gypsum, 'pieces of rock in which are embedded sea shells found in a gully near Naseby at an altitude of 2300ft [700m]', gum 'of a dark grey colour, hard, and very brittle', moa bones, blocks of sandstone, a copy of the London *Times* of 3 October 1798 with an account of the battle of the Nile, ironstone, curling trophies, the blades of a knife 'made from the prongs of a sluice fork', a chair, six bottles of gooseberry wine, a 150-year old engraving of Sir Philip Sidney, and Miss Packham's white counterpane, 'excellently worked'.

What would our district assemble now if there were to be another exhibition, and two bays for the Maniototo? Wild apples off trees grown from cores tossed from passing trains, seedling kōwhai trees, bales of wool (merino, Perendale), meat, and milk from down the valley where the tussocks and native grasses have disappeared, along with a mudbrick cottage and the settlers' trees. Instead, the giant irrigators turn and turn.

Lucerne in huge bales, not sheaves; soy flat whites and raw lemon slice from the café in a mudbrick cottage, once home to a family of ten. Novels, memoirs, history books, poetry, wire strainers and waratahs from Hayes Engineering, woven garments, props from movie sets (hobbit ears and a cowboy hat), schist blocks and pavers, garlic, saffron, honey, logs of pine, six bottles of raspberry-flavoured kombucha, turnips, peonies, wildflowers, an oil painting in the style of Gaugin of a man scything, lycra cycling outfits, electric bikes. A conch shell.

Path two

In August a storm brings snow to our valley. The hills crackle with white. I take the track up onto the ridgeline. The wind stirs the snow from the rocks and the thorns of matagouri so that it feels like it's snowing again, flakes brushing my arms though the sky is blue and clear.

The tors are vivid in the light, the lichens orange, sage-green, yellow-green, gold, the rock a warm grey and the snow luminous. The matagouri is adorned with white, its thorns clasping the ice, and the native grasses, half-buried in snow, thrust their gold fronds upwards.

Climbing the hill it was as warm as spring, but up here the wind is icy on my cheeks and lips. In the far distance the Old Woman and Old Man ranges are slick with snow. Clouds blur the tops, and I can only imagine how much bleaker it is at those heights, the wind unfettered, not even matagouri to crouch behind for shelter and the tors so towering they offer more threat than comfort. Unlike the house-sized rocks tumbled here, gathered in with *Coprosma propinqua* and muehlenbeckia, where there are small sheltered places in the sun to rest though my boots are deep in snow. A hawk sweeps silently over the rocks. Somewhere a magpie calls, and from far below comes the sound of a car, its wheels crunching over the packed ice on the tarseal. Yet even here, where the village is in view, I feel a frisson of fear at the wind and cold, at the distance still to go to reach home and the warmth of fire. Over the Dunstans and Blackstone Hill large clouds gather, tawny and dense with rain or snow, moving over the sky towards me.

Mt Ida Chronicle, 29 July 1893

… the weather, which is beastly – frost, snow and ice reigning supreme, making roads almost impassable, and effectually ending all mining and farming pursuits for the time being … Our school is at present closed up for a brief space on account of the severe weather. The greater portion of the scholars having to come from Rough Ridge and Ida Burn, a distance of three miles [5km] over a rough mountain track (and many of them young children) it is not to be wondered that attendance is meagre from those places.

Which way did the children go? Trevor points across the valley, tells us to walk up the fence line behind the poplars, where that tractor is mowing lucerne. His own father, at five years of age, climbed that way to school.

Neighbour Jo and I find the gate, walk behind the poplars and through a grove of elder trees blooming white. The hill stretches up to the tors. The wild shrubs on the slopes are flowering too: briar rose with sprinklings of pink flowers, the five heart-shaped petals shading to white, then yellow, then bronze stamens. Later, in autumn, I'll fill my pockets with the rosehips for oil. The thorned matagouri has its sweet, innocuous white flowers, and muehlenbeckia, the small-leafed pōhuehue, ripples over rocks, fence line and matagouri, its long wiry strands adorned with leaves. It too is in bloom, with small creamy-green flowers. In autumn its berries will swell to hold a black seed, juicy and palatable. The fruits were popular with Māori children, according to botanist William Colenso, writing in 1878.

There is native broom (desert broom, butterfly broom, or variously tawao, mākaka, maukoro or tainoka) with its strange, flattened green stalks, like a two-dimensional cactus. Sheep and rabbits have chewed the stems of some plants, leaving them bleached and fibrous so it looks as if they're flowering white too.

It's a steady climb upwards on a warm early summer's day. The vista opens out onto a wider ridge, and soon we can't see the gravelled road below us. The ridge must be kilometres wide. Hope begins to fade of finding a 125-year-old track that guided children among the tors. We think we see a line of cairns in the distance, but they too are tors. Which gully should we follow? Which track between the tarns and ponds and bogs, the shallow and damp hollows rimmed by rushes? I imagine a five-year-old clambering here in a group of children, in mist and sleet and wind and blazing heat, each towering rock a wonder for the imagination.

Jo and I climb up onto a rock and down again, peer into crevasses for moa bones, find hidden ferns, a yellow flower like a lily (bulbinella, commonly known as Māori onion), the skeleton of a magpie-sized bird, the dried hide and bones of a cow. Anywhere there could be quartz or bones or rare plants or some remnant of past lives.

Of all those who could have walked across this ridge – the early Māori, the gold miners, the shepherds – it is the children we know for sure came this way. Up and over a ridgeline, through tussock and matagouri and the damp gullies, down to the valley to Maruimato School, roll of twenty-five. Did they run that last stretch?

Moa once thrived here. Ran from the aim of hunters or the threat of flame. At the foot of Rough Ridge, 'scarcely a hole could be dug without some of the remains being exposed … bones and fragments of egg shells in great numbers were laid bare by the plough'. So wrote sheep farmer W.D. Murison in 1911. 'Scattered through the ovens were rude chert implements, many of which bore signs of having been used … knives … a cleaver … and fragments of polished stone implements.'

There's a late spring flush of grass on the hill. The lambs are half as big as their mothers and tolerant of us moving through the rocks where they are resting, the grass springy and vigorous and green. Somewhere beside us are the ghosts of children that were – children laughing, running, tired, sulky, curious. Their strong legs, knapsacks on their backs, oatcakes in their pockets, their hands chafed from milking, their stomachs warm with porridge and milk, the sun rising in their eyes.

Paradise ducks fly overhead honking. Jo and I walk past another tarn on the way home, the wind from the east blowing at our backs. As we pass the pond the air is suddenly old with the windblown smell of mud and wet rock and grass. Behind us, but not for our eyes this time, the stacked stone cairns parents made for their children to mark the safe track in a landscape of rocks and silence.

'There was always Lion Rock. You don't know it? I thought everyone knew Lion Rock.' Claire Becker grew up here, spent her childhood exploring

Rough Ridge. We meet at the Clyde Railhead Community Eco-Nursery, volunteers potting up native seedlings for planting in the wild. 'You go up the hill past the pines, to the right,' she tells me. 'The rock like a lion sitting down. It's where we went for family picnics, where we explored … Or we'd go to the old stone mill, though we weren't supposed to, and climb in the bread ovens. Or through the bull paddock and up to the Rock Gardens. We'd bounce on springy plant, muehlenbeckia, explore the stones … You have to go to Lion Rock.'

The hillside the children called the Rock Gardens is the site of the early Māori flint quarry: twenty hectares of silcrete or sarsen stone on a slope above our village. Jill Hamel describes the site in *The Archaeology of Otago*:

> Pits, usually 2–3m across and about 25cm deep, marked where unweathered silcrete had been quarried. Piles of good fine-grained material were stacked nearby, with cores and flakes strewn down a sunny slope.

> An area 6 x 10m of flaking floor was excavated, and over 14,000 flakes and cores removed for analysis and 'jig-saw' reconstruction. Analysis showed that large blocks had been quartered beside the quarry hole, elongated pieces carried away to a nearby working floor, where the cortex was flaked off and a platform shaped. Rough flakes and blades were removed to form a fluted core which might have been carried away or else further worked so that sets of blades could be struck off.

> On the basis of the flake technology present, the site was worked during the 13th and 14th centuries, since similar tools appear in coastal sites, such as the well-dated layers at Shag River Mouth.

Living here, it sometimes seems as if this place has always been a farming and trucking community, rather than what it is: a place where people have come for centuries in different guises. One night at a community meeting, newcomers to the village sat on one side of the long tables, established residents and landowners on the other. Were we newcomers outsiders? Or was it just a perception that night, the way we sat, the width of wood between us?

We are all subject to change in our lives. Change that drives us here, change that leads us away. We are all part of a long line of outsiders who have come here, like the moa hunters or the railway builders. Those who lived in what they could build: homes made of rushes or sods, a cave or tent, houses of earth, of timber and stone. It doesn't matter what convention dictates or whether we follow it or not. It doesn't matter how static we think life is or whether we think we have control. We are part of a wider story – wider than we imagine.

We don't know what the earth will unfold for us. We don't know the stories our own bodies hold for us, or how soon or far off those stories will end. It behoves us, I think, to wonder instead at how we are connected – through blood, through friendship, through place, through proximity.

Some people we choose in our lives and some we don't, yet here we are under a sky we have chosen together, under rain, snow, cloud shadow, warmth. What makes us a community? Not by being the same. Not just by being born here. Our hearts make us a community. The way we choose, in the end, to honour what is common among us: our need to live, to be recognised for who we are, and to respect and be protected by this land.

We are all trying to make sense of our story. And time is short.

Otago Witness, 18 January 1890 ('Letters from Little Folk')

After a while we took the old school track, and walked over the hill, and how delightful it was. We left home about 8 o'clock every morning, and were generally early for school. I had to milk four cows night and morning, but, nevertheless, I always enjoyed the walk to school. Rising at five o'clock, I would light the fire, and then start milking operations. How pleasant it was milking in the calm mornings 'neath the trees, while the birds sang merrily overhead. The cows milked and calves fed, I prepared for school, and then had breakfast. At this meal my brother always joined me, for he had no work to do, and always lay in bed till breakfast time. Soon we started our walk and in a short time reached the top of Rough Ridge. What a view meets our eyes! In front of us lay the White Sow Valley, with farms dotted here and there. Large green paddocks broke the monotony of scrub and tussock. Away in the distance may be seen Ranfurly and Hamiltons. One can get a splendid view of the Maniototo Plain, fringed on the far side with diggings. Turning again, we get a splendid view of Ida Valley and surroundings. Along each side of the valley are farms, with their cluster of trees. Directly in front is the township of Hills Creek, while at the far end of the valley lies the Ida Valley Station and various farms. As we descend we see our mates waiting, so we hurry …

Path three

There are two obstacles and therefore a choice to make on the path to Lion Rock. Go up the fence line safely and negotiate the electric fence, or go through the bull paddock inhabited by a brawny, huge-shouldered chestnut bull standing ten metres from the gate.

Brian chooses the electric fence hazard. I stand looking at the bull, who looks back at me from under his Neanderthal forehead. He begins to paw at the ground with one hoof and swing his tail. I choose the bull.

I'm sure he's the same bull Barry has told me about: 'He won't worry you; he's got other things on his mind.' I climb the gate and stride up the fence line. The bull begins to bellow. When I turn back he's still pawing there, dust flicking from his hoof, his eyes on some other horizon.

Lion Rock – which one? The tor on the ridgeline gradually defines itself as we climb higher, becomes a shaggy-maned lion sitting atop a large rock. The path, as always, further and more twisting than I'd imagined.

On the slopes there are plants piled upon plants: briar rose dominating matagouri, wiry pōhuehue climbing over both of them, native broom poking out the side. The air smells sweet with briar petals and warm grass, the hillside drying out after days of rain and now sun. Even the native broom is blooming; small white and purple folded flowers smelling of peas.

We circle the base of the tor. Would children have climbed it? The answer is clear at the back where a low sloping rock allows us to climb steadily, negotiating the spikes of wild Spaniard till we are standing on the lion's mane. The view is clear all the way down the valley to the Hector Mountains.

I wonder what it is I am trying to achieve – coming at Rough Ridge in summer, in snow, searching for tracks, for rocks, wondering what has been lost here: kahikatea and Hall's tōtara, tussock, moa, weka, children.

Perhaps I want to recapture the joy of wandering. Perhaps I want to bring my grandchildren here. Lion Rock! Perhaps I want to remember how rocks and shrubs are somehow magical – to be named and clambered on. To remember that facet of imagination which is nothing to do with craft or procrastination or disappointment. Perhaps it is all about wonder.

On the last stretch of slope is the ancient site of the silcrete mine, the boulders pink and gold and white under starbursts of lichen. Boulders tumbled under a pine, perched on schist, embedded in clay and tufty grass, the slabs and hunks scattered.

Wairua-ā-pō. Rough Ridge.

If the veil of time lifted, there would be strong forearms guiding the rock, the ringing of tools, stone against stone, voices in the air, the smell of sweat and dust and minerals hot in the sun.

Beyond a flowering elder tree a tangle of the 'springy plant', muehlenbeckia, so thick and wide I think maybe this is where the children came to explore. I crouch down to peer through curtains of leaves. There are sarsen rocks so rounded and plentiful and tumbled it is as if a river once flowed here and left its boulders behind. I part the curtain of wiry branches and climb through into a space secret and inexplicable, the moss and lichen-covered boulders in a network of leaves, heaped and stretching up the hill.

At home again, through my window I can see the pine on the hill but not the elder with the secret entrance beside it. The shrubs on the slope are grey and green shapes now. I shut my eyes to recall the smell of grass, of briar rose and broom, and the warm flanks of rocks that have been there since before any of us thought to raise our eyes to the hills.

I think it is not enough to gaze at a mountain or hill, nor desire to climb it, without bringing awareness of what the land is in itself. Meeting it there. Not wondering what it can give you – rosehips, grass, elderflowers, the view – but meeting it in the way I came to learn from the river: as its own being with the right to thrive.

This season farmers have harvested one crop of lucerne already. The spring has been wet and mostly mild. A three-crop year then? But no, a farmer tells me, if the rain doesn't continue, the regrowth won't happen. It's not a given. The land will yield bounty or not. They know this, scanning the sky.

A path worn by sheep, a narrow track between rock and the pronged branches of the matagouri (shelter for birds and lizards) and the springy mass of pōhuehue (home to twenty-eight species of invertebrates), the plants protecting those that pollinate and so ensuring each other's existence; a microcosm of a world in balance that we can walk right by without a thought, immersed in our solitude. But even solitude is a human presumption, according to American writer Barbara Kingsolver: 'Every quiet step is thunder to beetle life underfoot.'

What is it then, about being here, about these paths onto Rough Ridge – onto any ridge? That they only make the deepest sense if we know where we are and what we are among.

'I have had the privilege of spending my life kneeling before plants,' says American biologist Robin Wall Kimmerer in her article 'Speaking of Nature'. 'I am always in awe, and always in relationship.' What we need now, she says, is 'humility and ecological compassion'.

A few days later I am in Southland, writing by a window overlooking the coast, when I am called by the shout of 'Dolphins!' There they are, a pod breaching and sinking in the blue-grey sea. We run out the door in pyjamas, the grandchildren barefoot, up the gravel road, over the stile, down through the lupins and long grass and up the shaggy path to the rocks overlooking Taramea, Howells Point. A pod of maybe fifteen rare bottle-nosed dolphins below us, and on the rocks people standing and watching, on the road cars pulled over, people holding up cellphones. 'They're breaching right in front of us!' And the dolphins moving further and further away, circling dark swarms of seaweed, arcing and diving. We stand transfixed, in awe, aching for relationship.

Across the Whited Fields

The first day

In a twilight street
a small girl laughing.

The red and yellow flowers
profuse, inhale the air.

We want to hold your name,
Polly, dancing in the rain,

Polly, skipping down the street.
Sometimes the world bequeaths

then takes away the one to whom
our hearts will open wide.

We were beguiled. You are so innocent
so innocent so innocent.

THERE IS A LOCH in the Cairngorm mountains of Scotland, Loch Avon,
where the waters are so clear, so bright, that after wading into them and
being confronted by the unexpected depth and clarity, Nan Shepherd wrote
in *The Living Mountain* of 'a gulf of brightness so profound that the mind
stopped'. When I set out to write of place, of the mountains and streams in
my valley in Central Otago, the tor-serrated hills, and the village where over
the years many people have arrived to live, I did not think I would come to
write of the loss of one of them, a young woman so bright in spirit it was as
if we had an innocent set down among us.

How can I write of Polly, who was broken by the world, without thinking of that clear loch in the land her family set out from, where water pours over 'grim bastions' yet carries no sediment? A waterfall, Shephard wrote, that seems 'to distill and aerate the water so that the loch far below is sparkling clear'.

Polly had long purple hair, black-rimmed glasses and an array of wild and coloured clothing. ('That lady with the awesome clothes,' nine-year-old Jude said.) Polly walking down the one street in our village in scarf and shorts and steampunk tights and red sunglasses, wide-eyed at the hills around her, black labrador Lola at her side.

Into this rural community had come first one poet then others; people seeking community or quietness, those who stayed in their garden or those who leaned on their gates to talk. Then there was Polly in tartan and bangles, skipping down the street. She'd just turned forty yet had the spirit of a child, dazzling in her beauty, innocent even of the machinations of agriculture.

One night at the pub, sheep farmer Ken tried to explain to her the incidence of sheep measles in lambs, caused by untreated dogs. 'When we cut the lamb open …'

'You kill your lambs?' said Polly, shocked.

'Well, we didn't know we had a problem with sheep measles until we opened …'

'You kill your lambs?' she asked again, and Ken stopped, slightly bewildered.

'It's all right,' Polly said, recovering herself. 'My dad told me I have to tread lightly in the village. I'll zip it. I won't say one more word about killing lambs.'

'Just don't feed your dog raw meat,' said Ken.

'Oh, that's ok,' Polly said. 'My dog's vegetarian.'

'She told me she was training her dog in five languages,' another farmer, Richard Anderson, told me. 'It made me smile. And I heard her, too, when her dog went to run in my gate: "Nein, Lola, nein!"' He stopped. 'I feel like we've been robbed,' he said. 'All the years we could have had Polly in our lives.'

Polly lived in a studio over the fence from me while she waited for her house to be built, and when I texted *come for a cuppa* she would lope up the grass, a coffee already in her hands, fingerless gloves on. Sometimes I gave her healing – reiki or hand acupuncture – for the pain she lived with: a broken neck, rods fused in her spine, a shattered ankle. Even to walk pained her. And sometimes she would give healings alongside me, sitting on the verandah in the sun, sending her bright compassionate thoughts to people she didn't know yet continued, she told me, to hold in her heart.

How can a person live in a village such a short time and yet affect people so much?

'I didn't know her well,' the shopkeeper Helen said, her voice breaking. 'But I loved her.'

'Heartbreaking, just … heartbreaking,' the builder Justin said, standing on the pad of Polly's home, the first wall raised.

'I wrote her name in the concrete pad,' I told him.

'I saw it,' he said. 'Just there, almost under the window.'

On that night, the concrete pad almost dry, I'd gone over at twilight and stood beside the shimmering floor, a wide expanse like a page where a house would be written. I'd imagined a window where Polly could sit and look at the mountains, then had picked up a small stick and written her name into the cooling concrete. When Justin pointed out the scrawl in the hardened floor, Polly and a heart, I realised I had missed the window by a centimetre. And now her name is forever under the wall, etched in the floor as she is in our memories.

Those waters of the Avon, springing from that clear loch. The clarity of the waters 'so absolute that there is no image for them,' Nan Shepherd wrote. 'They are elemental transparency … their quality is natural, but is found so seldom in its absolute state that when we do so find it, we are astonished.'

We were astonished by Polly.

'She was a dreamy child,' her father Mike Riddell said. 'Introverted and kind and innocent.'

When Polly was eleven she was raped.

By fourteen she was a morphine addict.

At sixteen she was on the streets.

Her father spoke these truths at her funeral that we may know the courage with which Polly lived.

('The hardest challenge in life is always going to be the fight within yourself' – an abuse survivor.)

At sixteen, her first suicide attempt. Polly threw herself from a six-metre wall onto concrete. 'A miracle patient who survived,' her doctor described her. Now the pain she felt inside was externalised.

At twenty-eight her neck was broken in a head-on car crash. Polly in her hospital bed, eyes closed, with neck brace and screws.

'She somehow kept her beautiful innocence and sense of wonder through everything,' her father said. He wrote:

> Rosemary said you were practising
> and would get better
> but you won't ever get better
> than you always were
> alive with love, alive with joy,
> alive

The hawk of depression so close she could see the pinions of its feathers, at the same time hearing the clarion calls of bellbirds or the froth of chirping sparrows in the willows. She carried a handbag full of packets of drugs, a multitude of painkillers for the comfort of knowing help was at hand when she needed it. Polly in her tutu, her hair in braids, almost a rainbow.

The long shadow of sexual abuse took Polly with an unexpected and unexplained overdose. Child sexual abuse victims 'are at increased risk of both suicide and accidental fatal overdose', an Australian study found. The mean age of death from accidental overdose: thirty-one. These are events that are studied, linked, numbered, given percentages. It's unmistakable, the possible outcome.

Polly wrote to her father:

> I am excited for our future!
> To live next door to you!
> To settle our bones, adventure,
> Together
> In that magical wee village, Oturehua,
> Wrapped around by giant hugging mountains.

All the stars she wondered at and the glory of the sunset skies, all the love she had for her father and mother and sister and brother, and the love they had for her – in that one instant could not hold her, though we longed for her to be safe.

There are ten of us in the village whose children have grown and live away.

'I think our hearts filled up for Polly because we are all parents and don't have our own children here,' our neighbour Alison said. 'We wanted to protect her.'

Blackstone Hill Cemetery is a small square graveyard on the flank of a rising hill. It's edged by hawthorn, with cast-iron gates at the front and a view across fields to the Hawkduns and Mt Ida. The Home Hills are to the left, and far in the distance to the right is the long rugged length of Rough Ridge. One warm dry Saturday morning in February, eight months before, Brian Turner and I had driven there to weed graves. We weren't able to make the public event the next day, when twenty people would turn up to tidy and garden. Instead, we had the headstones and the birdsong to ourselves.

We fetched spades and gloves and cardboard boxes for the weeds from the car and chose the first row, on the left, to begin. Here in the cemetery wild flowers thrived, especially hollyhocks. They sprouted between graves, in graves, on the edges of graves, soaring in this sheltered space, their blooms scarlet and purple. Cleavers ran wild over the ground and surged in sticky green waves over the graves' dividing fences. There were sweet peas with purple blooms, yellow stonecrop, white daisies, and the weeds – dandelion, yarrow, thistle, dock. Where to start? Not with the hollyhocks. Unlike urban cemeteries, which are either a concreted city of headstones or a mown green lawn, nature has taken a hold here. Flowers come back each year and bloom where they will, bringing their exuberance to an enclosure of etched names and grief.

We pulled out dock, yarrow, long rank ryegrass and cleavers and left the sweet peas, the oxeye daisies and the hollyhocks. Each grave had its own low fence around it, sometimes ironwork, sometimes a raised concrete edge. Before stepping onto each grave – for instance, Charles Brown, died 24 June 1917, or Fanny McKeeman, died September 1908, aged thirty-eight – I read the name aloud, acknowledging the person we were visiting as if knocking on the door to let them know we'd arrived. Brian and I worked side by side on the graves, which were like small houses with their gardens set in a small grassed street. And I came to understand, head down, shaking a clump of soil from a dock before tossing it into the cardboard box, smoothing over the soil, patting it down by the hollyhocks, that here was a community – the ones who had lived before us. This was the small township they dwelt in now, with skylarks and paradise ducks overhead, sparrows in the hedgerows, and sometimes plovers and pied oyster catchers in the green across the road.

None of the dead are ours, but in some sense they belong to all of us, for we all know grief and its precursor, love.

'I see you left the hollyhocks alone,' organiser Judy Beck said when I rang her that night. 'That's good. There's always someone in the group who yanks them out.'

In that golden time of flowers, Polly and her dad Mike had driven up to visit the newly weeded cemetery.

'She turned around and around with her phone, filming the graves and the views for Instagram,' Mike told me. How I wished I'd followed her on Instagram and seen the land and names and flowers through her eyes.

Instead, we arrive at the cemetery again in October and it for is Polly that we are here. The peace flags on the cemetery fence have faded to grey. I wish they were pink and purple with sparkles for her. The white hearse rolls slowly through the gates. Ken Gillespie, now sextant and solemn in black jacket and trousers, is there to meet her. As Polly's friend he has been responsible for her grave and has dug it with farmers Graeme McKnight and Bruce Blakie. The straight sides of the hole reveal the layers of soil, the striations of geology. No fake grass here to cover up what is real; the clean-smelling home of earth.

Ken has laid hay in the bottom of the grave. Afterwards, he will cover the poignant mound with hay and lay the flowers upon it. Tucking Polly in.

All day it has been hot, sweltering for spring. That long hot drive back from the service in Dunedin city to the green of Blackstone Hill. As we gather in the cemetery, blue-black clouds rise over the hill and the hawthorns. Mike stands beside the coffin, his hand reaching for her lid ('with you, with you,' he wrote afterwards, 'always with you/ in a home made of love/ without any roof').

Mike has once been a pastor. He knows the words of the service, but in his mouth, and in this place, from father to daughter, that age-old phrase takes on a poignant gravity: 'Earth to earth, ashes to ashes ...' We step forward, but not with soil. We cast streamers and coloured paper and confetti into that earthen bed.

'Knowing Polly, there'll be some sign,' Mike says, and at that moment the clouds let loose the rain upon us.

A week after the funeral Judy Beck rings again, this time for a working bee to weed the garden at the domain. A wonderful gardener herself, Judy is now in a wheelchair. She knows the village and the village gardens. She knows what needs to be done.

Seven of us turn up, all women on this roster. The garden is a tangled area under two trees – a mauve weeping crab apple in full bloom and a flowering cherry with branches of delicate white. Under the trunks, cleavers again, and dock, and ryegrass with roots so thick our spades can barely daunt it.

'One of these trees was planted for the little girl who drowned up at Beckers' coal pits, about twenty years ago,' Wendy Blakie says, for there are five of us who've been here fewer than twenty years. But Wendy remembers and so does Carol, the previous publican from the hotel across the road from Beckers Transport.

The publicans at that time had a young daughter, Jacy. The local children knew not to skate on the frozen coal pits.

'The ice in the coal pit is not like other ice,' Barry Becker told me. 'It's slushy. It doesn't freeze the same.'

'If you ever do fall through ice,' farmer Murray McKnight told me, 'don't swim towards the light. You have to swim towards the dark. The light is the ice above your head. The dark is your only way through.'

Seven-year-old Jacy went with a younger boy who'd lived in the village only a few years. Neither of them knew the danger. They slipped away from the hotel to skate on the transport company's frozen wash pond, formerly William Clucas's coal pit. Jacy fell through the ice. The younger boy ran to the closed garage then back to stand beside the ice, where he waited for Jacy to surface again.

We listen to our village tragedy, bending and stooping under the boughs, tugging at the ryegrass and its roots, tenacious through droughts and ice-packed winters and all the long years since a young girl's classmates had stood here by a sapling tree.

A four-wheel drive pulls up on the roadside. Ken, on his way to check progress on the village walkway, perhaps wondering why there is a bustle of women and tools under the two trees.

'Have you found Jacy's plaque?' is the first thing he says. 'It should be here, under her tree.'

'It's not here,' Wendy says 'There's a hole where it should have been, because I tripped in it. Bob Bellamy's taken it home to fix and set on a new post.'

'Which tree is hers?' I ask.

'That one, the white blossom,' Ken says. And he tells the story again, of the small girl and the tragedy of silence.

On any weekday outside the store there'll be a farmer's ute with dog on the back, a truck driver with high-vis jacket, or villagers, all come for their morning mail or paper or coffee. Perhaps Pete Ryan, biking home no-handed while he reads the paper's headlines. Today, Armistice Day, there we are again, villagers, visitors, all in good clothing under the sudden hot sun: Paula in a frock, Annie from Hayes in full Victorian gear, the farmers in pressed check shirts. Ken and Graeme Male hand out poppies. Polly's sister has come with Polly's dog. The piper stands and plays as we sit in chairs arranged on the footpath outside the store.

'Do they know I'm reading a poem too?' I whisper to Brian in the front row. I'd just arrived back from visiting grandchildren.

'Yes. I told Trevor Beck,' Brian whispers back.

The fine weather is a surprise and a bounty for us. Last week there'd been rain and snow. Trevor steps up to the front. He's a retired farmer, a gentleman, much involved in the community. ('Though this is the last thing I'm organising,' he says later. 'I'm getting too forgetful.')

'A hundred years ago on the twelfth of November (we were a day behind the world),' Trevor begins, 'the locals were gathered here in the hall in front of us, waiting for news. First, the telegraph boy arrived' – and up runs Ollie from next door, long-legged and grinning, and hands Trevor the telegram. 'News is coming.'

There's the sound of a throbbing motorbike. Pete Ryan rides into view in full army kit – Trevor's tin hat and kitbag, someone's shirt, twill trousers, even putties. Pete runs to Trevor. 'Good news!' he calls with his trademark wide grin. He hands Trevor a newspaper and he reads:

'The Germans have surrendered! The war is over!' Caught up in the drama, we stand up from our seats on the footpath and yell.

For those gathered back then, their husbands and sons still so far away, it must have been like that moment scrambling up Mt Ida through cloud, when we walked out of the swirl and mist onto rock shining in the sun, the high flanks of the mountain and the ridgeline tors clear, the tussock gold; while below, what was once claggy and unfathomable had become a soft and luminescent land.

It would feel something like peace.

There were some who came home and wouldn't talk about it, like the grandfathers in Brian's poem which he stands to read, 'Memories of war':

> 'We fought because we had to,
> it was as simple as that for most of us,'
> and, my father's father added,
> 'Heroics were commonplace. But no
> more questions. Go outside and play.'

Not for those rheumy, shuttered-eyed men the memory of guns in putrid air.

In the valley the men came home to the farms or the railway. But not to the school – the teacher was dead and his fiancée bereft. And the other sons who didn't make it – from the Somme, from leg wounds, from meningitis – changed or gone, we remember them. To help us, there are rows of young faces in sepia on the board in front of us.

When I stand up to read my poem there is a lull in the traffic going by. There are only the words, and the upturned faces of people I know, and the moment of shared poignancy in our lives still cradled with grief, still staccatoed by fear and fractured by wrongdoings and missed opportunities for grace.

And now it ends

(for the Ida Valley, Armistice Day)

The frost that cowed the blooms was just the start –
there was hail and snow and thunder yet to come.
And now it ends, we hold the fallen to our heart.

In the dawn, the chill winds laid their mark.
The harvest of our children had begun.
The frost that cowed the blooms was just the start.

They were taken from our yard and from our hearth,
those who'd bloomed, and those whose blooming was to come.
And now it ends, we hold the fallen to our heart.

The art of war was never any art
for us, when winter's shadows paled the sun.
The frost that cowed the blooms was just the start.

No more the blackened leaves, the silent lark,
nor rubble in the fields concealing limbs,
for now it ends, we hold the fallen to our heart.

We let them go, and in this way, we played our part.
Across the tracks of snow, we call them home.
The frost that cowed the blooms was just the start
and now it ends, we hold the fallen to our heart.

There are sandwiches and cakes across the road at the pub. Time to sit in
the sun and talk. And the mountains are still there, and the hills and the
tors. On Rough Ridge, the wild briar blooming.

'I thank you for always breaking the bleak times,' Polly wrote in a poem to
her dad,

With ease, faith and that deep, guttural laugh we share.
Throughout … the beers with Grampa at the Waterloo,

The phone calls daily, later when he loosened his grip,
Or I lost mine,
You continue to build me up, bringing such light to my
Wounded soul.

It's meant to be spring but there's snow again, horizontal in the wind from the south. At the cemetery the hawthorns are frothed with blossom. Their boughs reach to the ground. They are like bridal veils, so full of their own white in a white landscape. Hawthorn blossoming on three sides and one elder tree, with its open palms of white flowers.

Snow lies between the graves and along the headstones, but not on Polly's warmer soil. I lay a branch of hawthorn blossom next to the cross adorned with her greenstone necklace. When I stand up, another woman with flowers in her hand is making her way between the graves. It's Becky Reid, from the village café.

'Who are you visiting?' I call.

'Polly,' she calls back. She's brought daisies and red peonies from her garden. She lays them next to the hawthorn blossom. We stand there at the foot of Polly's grave, silent for a minute, two bundled women in the wintry air.

When the snows melt, the Ida Burn will roll and tumble in high spate, ploughing banks and broom and young willows into its waters. No-one can predict these things: how far the river will rise, how long the snow will lie on the flanks of Mt Ida or the drought last when it comes, as it will, burning the land with gold. All these things the land submits to, and survives.

'In every sunrise and snowfall/ we will know you, love you,' Mike wrote of Polly,

> you are the valley
> that has cleft us raw
> be at home, sweet daughter
> be delirious with joy
> be aching with beauty
> be, just be.

When Becky and I walk past the graves, the stories are in the stone and in the words we've heard. We pause to consider them: this young woman who died in childbirth; this young man with a red poppy on his headstone, killed in action; this loved husband unexpectedly lost. We submit because that is all that can be done.

The hollyhocks have sprung from cracks and graves again, their leathery leaves wide open to the snow. The oxeye daisies are in full bud, the sweet pea tendrils sweep over the wrought iron. Nothing is in bloom yet, but everything is ready. Those whose names are listed are inaccessible to us now: we have only the memories we hold. The love is in the care, in the extra turf Ken has placed on Polly's grave because of the rain, in the plastic daisies spinning in the wind, in the handwritten message on a grandmother's wooden cross: 'You are the best grandmother ever.'

Two paddocks over, a farmer is shifting sheep. The dogs bark and bark. The farmer's voice is audible but not the words, until the wind shifts.

'Here Bess! Here Bess!' across the whited fields.

Beyond the long sweep of the valley, the mountains rise.

References by Essay

Becoming Something Other

The title is from Chris Knox's song 'Becoming Something Other', from the album *Beat* (2000)

Where there is no pit sand – Vitruvius: www.gutenberg.org/files/20239/20239-h/20239-h.htm

It is essential – Paul Oliver: https://epdf.pub/vernacular-architecture-in-the-21st-century-theory-education-and-practice.html

How do you know – Jillian Sullivan, 'Choosing', in *Parallel* (Wellington: Steele Roberts, 2014), p. 62

Life is an unremitting series – Joseph Campbell, *The Hero with a Thousand Faces* (London: Fontana Press, 1993), p. 60

The proper business of living – Talbot Mundy, *I Say Sunrise* (London: Andrew Dakers, 1947)

The great truth – Marilynne Robinson, *When I Was a Child I Read Books* (London: Hachette Digital, 2012), p. 33

Rough walls become smooth – Jillian Sullivan, 'Lime Plaster', in *takahē 84*, April 2015

Want is a thing – Barbara Kingsolver, *High Tide in Tucson* (London: Faber & Faber, 2011), p. 12

Between Lands

What are they going to do when they get there? – Theo Chaisson: www.independent.co.uk/news/world/americas/time-almost-up-island-louisiana-sinking-into-the-sea-american-indians-coastal-erosion-isle-de-jean-a8280401.html

Ancient Land

The loveliest places of all – Brian Turner, 'Deserts, for instance', in *Just This* (Wellington: Victoria University Press, 2009), p. 34

One must simplify it – Wendell Berry, *The Long-Legged House* (Berkeley: Counterpoint, 2012), p. 112

If we have no clear idea – Robert Michael Pyle, in Nathaniel Brodie, Charles Goodrich and Frederick Swanson (eds), *Forest Under Story: Creative inquiry in an old-growth forest* (Washington: University of Washington Press, 2016), p. 19

The Ohau was a boisterous, belligerent river – Brian Turner, *Somebodies and Nobodies: Growing up in an extraordinary sporting family* (Auckland: Random House, 2002), p. 202

The desertification of Central Otago – Susan Walker, Alan F. Mark and J. Bastow Wilson, 'The vegetation of Flat Top Hill: An area of semi-arid grassland/shrubland in Central Otago, New Zealand', *New Zealand Journal of Ecology*, vol. 19, no. 2 (1995), pp. 175–94: https://newzealandecology.org/nzje/1977

This plant is small, simple, delicate – Isla Burgess, *The Biophilic Garden: Connecting people, plants and inscape* (Cromwell: Viriditus Publishing, 2017), p. 31

This stuff makes gorse look like sheep's wool – Cameron Slater, Whale Oil: www.whaleoil.net.nz/tag/matagouri/

To see *into* the natural world – Michael Harlow, email to author

The Hawkdun Range

When people pay close attention – Charles Goodrich, in Brodie, Goodrich and Swanson (eds), *Forest Under Story*, p. 8

a commodity (for the gaze) – Aldo Leopold, *A Sand County Almanac* (New York: Oxford University Press, 1949), p. viii

It was a week before any word – *Otago Witness*, 2 September 1908

The insistent miner – Janet Cowan, *Down the Years in the Maniototo* (Whitcombe & Tombs and Otago Centennial Historical Committee, 1948), p. 150

[Tussock grassland] was important – *Otago Daily Times*, 31 December 2009

exploiter, shirker, weak-kneed quibbling – *Otago Daily Times*, 12 December 1916

significantly reduce the amount of irrigation – Conservation Reserve Enhancement Programme: https://dnr.nebraska.gov/sites/dnr.nebraska.gov/files/doc/surface-water/crep/annual-reports/CREPReport2019.pdf

In Search of Ancient New Zealand, Hamish Campbell and Gerard Hutching (Auckland: Penguin, 2007), p. 182

The way forward – Catherine Knight, *Beyond Manapouri: 50 years of environmental politics in New Zealand* (Christchurch: Canterbury University Press, 2018), p. 213

I believe we've almost poisoned our soil – Barry Becker, cited in Brian Turner, *Boundaries* (Auckland: Penguin Random House, 2015), p. 42

In Germany for instance – Knight, *Beyond Manapouri*, p. 146

We can be ethical only in relation – Leopold, *A Sand County Almanac*, p. 214

A Roof Over Our Heads

man was quite at home– Joseph Rykwert: www.hermitary.com/bookreviews/rykwert.html

Cycling with Bartali: A year in the valley

the light is like honey – Brian Turner, 'Place', in *All That Blue Can Be* (Dunedin: John McIndoe, 1989), p. 21

wind fierce out of the west – Jillian Sullivan, 'West Wind', in *The Unexpected Greenness of Trees* (Dunedin: Caselberg Press, 2016), p. 90

What's productive here – Brian Turner, 'Van Morrison in Central Otago', in *Beyond* (Dunedin: John McIndoe, 1992), p. 10

In the Midst of My True Life

Wind again – Jillian Sullivan, 'Molecular Knowhow', in *The Unexpected Greenness of Trees* (Dunedin: Caselberg Press, 2016), p. 86

I'm juggling fear and awe – Jillian Sullivan, 'Straw', in *Kiss Me Hardy*, issue 1, 2017

At Bollingen I am in the midst – C.G. Jung, *Memories, Dreams, Reflections* (New York: Random House, 1961), p. 225

Such an act is no mere vagary – Berry, *The Long-Legged House*, p. 92

be a warrior – Jillian Sullivan, 'Restraint', in *Press*, April 2015

Straw, timber and earth – Min Hall, 'Earth and straw bale: An investigation of their performance and potential as building materials in New Zealand', MA thesis, Victoria University of Wellington, 2012, p. 131

The largest reason – Ellen Jackson, 'Self reliance and earth building in New Zealand: A case-study of the struggle between sustainability and consumerism', MA thesis, University of Auckland, 2009, p. 174

up with the drill, the hammer – Jillian Sullivan, 'Summer with a Ladder', *takahē*, April 2015

In our wake – Kathleen Dean Moore in *Wild Comfort* (Canada: Trumpeter Books, 2010), p. 113

When I get up – Jillian Sullivan, unpublished poem

Barefoot Running

hope and grace – Brian Turner, 'Foretold', in *Elemental* (Auckland: Random House, 2012), p. 203

Woman may not be as abject as she appears – Debra Bergoffen, *The Philosophy of Simone de Beauvoir: Gendered phenomenologies, erotic generosities* (New York: State University of New York Press, 1997), p. 171

Diminished status can, in fact, sustain and inform – Akiko Busch, 'The invisiblity of older women': www.theatlantic.com/entertainment/archive/2019/02/akiko-busch-mrs-dalloway-shows-aging-has-benefits/583480/

No longer did she glimmer – Jillian Sullivan, *Myths and Legends: The gift of stories from our cultures* (Auckland: Pearson Education NZ, 2007), p. 86

Love, Loss and the Fraser Basin

There's gold – Jillian Sullivan, 'Jolly Fellow', unpublished poem

First, we have to – Ibid.

Even a brief glimpse – Dervla Murphy: www.theguardian.com/travel/2018/jan/24/
dervla-murphy-travel-writer-interview-full-tilt

This land's part of what's called nature – Brian Turner, 'Hard Luck, Nature', in *Inside
Outside* (Wellingon: Victoria University Press, 2011), p. 71

embracing and comprehending – Marcus Aurelius in Tamer Nashef, 'The idea of
progress: A comparative study': https://strangenotions.com/the-idea-of-progress-a-
comparative-study/

The likelihood is we won't – Turner, 'Hard Luck, Nature'

We shrink from change – Marcus Aurelius, *Meditations* (England: Penguin, 1995), p. 46

Every kind of passing – Grant Clauser, 'Carbon County Boulder Field', *Necessary Myths*
(Delaware: Broadkill River Press, 2013), p. 71

that stands on shoulders of sterner/ deeper woes – Jillian Sullivan, unpublished

Over Bendigo way – Sullivan, 'Jolly Fellow'

one of the main or leading reefs – *Tuapeka Times*, cited in John Breen, *Nicholson's Folly*
(Cambridge: Halcyon Press, 2017), pp. 28, 70

The Black Hills of Dakota – Doris Day

We are the Pilgrims, master – James Elroy Flecker, 'The Golden Road to Samarkand':
www.poetryatlas.com/poetry/poem/119/the-golden-road-to-samarkand.html

Coming out of the bush – Jillian Sullivan, unpublished poem

But will you pay us – Sullivan, 'Jolly Fellow'

'Salvation,' Aurelius wrote – Marcus Aurelius, *Meditations: A new translation, with an
introduction by Gregory Hays* (New York/Canada: Modern Library, 2002), loc. 2556
of 3061

Perhaps of all men – John E. Martin, *The Forgotten Worker: The rural wage earner in
nineteenth-century New Zealand* (Wellington: Bridget Williams Books, 1990), loc.
157

A glacier paused – Clauser, 'Carbon County Boulder Field', p. 71

The Art and Adventure of Subsistence

Subsistence Protection Affection – Emma Kidd, *First Steps to Seeing* (Edinburgh: Floris
Books, 2015), p. 145

[I]t is not just an inability – Kidd, *First Steps to Seeing*, p. 150

Through the eyes – Kidd, *First Steps to Seeing*, p. 151

There is something heroic – David Shields, *Reality Hunger: A manifesto* (London:
Hamish Hamilton, Penguin, 2010), p. 136

uncertainties, Mystery, doubts – Stephen Hebron, 'John Keats and "negative capability"':
www.bl.uk/romantics-and-victorians/articles/john-keats-and-negative-capability

Each of my books … has been met – Edward Abbey, *The Best of Edward Abbey* (New
York: Sierra Club Books, 1984), p. xi

Growing Closer

When the suffering of another creature – Leo Tolstoy, 'A Calendar of Wisdom', cited at: www.facebook.com/dovesnz/

I have been inside – Carl D. Scott: www.facebook.com/dovesnz/

It was just like snow – Donald Young: www.tvnz.co.nz/one-news/new-zealand/otago-farmers-label-new-virus-introduced-control-rabbits-complete-failure-v1

The rabbit problem – www.rnz.co.nz/news/country/312921/central-otago-rabbit-population-%27escalating%27

Through the process of paying focused and sustained attention – Daniel C. Wahl, '"Zarte Empirie": Goethean science as a way of knowing': https://medium.com/age-of-awareness/zarte-empirie-goethean-science-as-a-way-of-knowing-e1ab7ad63f46

The "humaneness" of a pest animal control method – https://pestsmart.org.au/animal-welfare/humaneness-assessment/rabbit/

When people tell me – Carl D. Scott: www.facebook.com/dovesnz/

Exact sensorial imagination – Wahl, 'Zarte Empirie'

Attention without feeling – Mary Oliver, *Our World* (New York: Penguin Random House, 2007), p. 71

Systematic practice of Goethean methodology – Wahl, 'Zarte Empirie'

The Primitive Hut

In the present rethinking – Joseph Rykwert, *On Adam's House in Paradise: The idea of the primitive hut in architectural history* (New York: Museum of Modern Art, 1972), p. 192

not enough to have a liking for architecture – Michel Foucault, *Discipline and Punish: The birth of the prison* (New York: Vintage, 1979), p. 139

for little or no cost – John and Gerry Archer, *Dirt Cheap: The mudbrick book* (Birregurra, Victoria: Compendium, 1976), p. 2

We found that many people – Archer and Archer, *Dirt Cheap*, p. 2

a thrifty balancing of cost and common sense – Vitruvius: www.gutenberg.org/files/20239/20239-h/20239-h.htm

The cost of a thing – Henry David Thoreau, *Works of Henry David Thoreau* (New York: Avenel Books, 1981), p. 34

Lifting Walls

Without reverence – Brian Turner, 'Declaration', in *Elemental* (Auckland: Random House, 2012), p. 148

Two carefully placed layers – Jill Hamel, *The Archaeology of Otago*: www.doc.govt.nz/Documents/science-and-technical/The_Achaeology_of_Otago_Jill_Hamel_WEB.pdf

To build a pyramid – May Sarton, 'Lifting Stone', in *Writings on Writing* (London: Women's Press), p. 23

The sods were stacked – Hamel, *The Archaeology of Otago*

There is a deep, pervasive satisfaction – Nan Shepherd, *The Living Mountain* (Edinburgh: Canongate Books, 2011), p. 82

What if a River Wants to Sing?

The scenic qualities of the Ahuriri – New Zealand Acclimatisation Societies: www.mfe.govt.nz/sites/default/files/media/A%20river.pdf

Tell the unspangled truth – Beth Kephart, *Strike the Empty* (Philadelphia: Juncture Workshops, 2019), p. 88

The reality is – Mike Joy, *Polluted Inheritance* (Wellington: Bridget Williams Books, 2015), p. 11

A technical report by Otago Regional Council – www.orc.govt.nz/media/2433/management-flows-for-aquatic-ecosystems-in-the-manuherikia-river-and-dunstan-creek-web.pdf

the courage to dam the rivers – Sir Tipene O'Regan speaking at Aspiring Conversations, 7 July 2019 (from private notes)

We have the world to live in – Wendell Berry: https://billmoyers.com/segment/wendell-berry-on-his-hopes-for-humanity/

A thing is right – Leopold, *A Sand County Almanac*, pp. 224–25

Healthy functioning ecosystems –Joy, *Polluted Inheritance*, p. 57

you know what the river is saying – Brian Turner, 'River Wind', in *All That Blue Can Be* (Dunedin: John McIndoe, 1989), p. 28

Blackstone Hill

I never saw a stick growing – Grahame Sydney, *Promised Land: From Dunedin to the Dunstan goldfields* (North Shore: Penguin, 2009), p. 140

On July 9 1869 – Janet Cowan in Judy Beck, *Blackstone Hill Cemetery: An A–Z of the families who lie there, 1864–1964* (Ōtūrehua: Judy Beck, 2017), p. 315

The moment that the auctioneer – Robert Gilkison in Beck, *Blackstone Hill*, p. 37

dim deepwood of massive and mossbound trees – Robert Michael Pyle in in Brodie, Goodrich and Swanson (eds), *Forest Under Story*, p. 17

to walk, observe, reflect and record their insights – Charles Goodrich in Brodie, Goodrich and Swanson (eds), *Forest Under Story*, pp. 7, 8

nobody/ knows how much time we have – Brian Turner in Brodie, Goodrich and Swanson (eds), *Forest Under Story*, p. 92

The long view – Charles Goodrich in Brodie, Goodrich and Swanson (eds), *Forest Under Story*, pp. 10, 11

Three Paths to Rough Ridge

The fruits were popular – Andrew Crowe, *Native Edible Plants of New Zealand* (Auckland: Hodder and Stoughton, 1990), p. 37

scarcely a hole could be dug – *Mt Ida Chronicle*, 25 August 1911

Pits, usually 2–3m across – Hamel, *The Archaeology of Otago*

Every quiet step is thunder – Barbara Kingsolver, *Prodigal Summer* (London: Faber and Faber, 2001), p. 3

I have had the privilege – Robin Wall Kimmerer, 'Speaking of Nature', *Orion*: https://orionmagazine.org/article/speaking-of-nature/

Across the Whited Fields

a gulf of brightness so profound – Nan Shepherd, *The Living Mountain* (Edinburgh: Canongate Books, 2011), p. 12

so absolute that there is no image – Shepherd, *The Living Mountain*, p. 3

The hardest challenge in life – *Otago Daily Times* (n.d.)

Child sexual abuse victims 'are at increased risk' – *Medical Journal of Australia*: www.mja.com.au/journal/2010/192/4/suicide-and-fatal-drug-overdose-child-sexual-abuse-victims-historical-cohort

We fought because we had to – Brian Turner, 'Memories of War', in *Footfall* (Auckland: Random House, 2005), p. 64

The frost that cowed the blooms – Jillian Sullivan, 'And Now it Ends', *North & South*, 14 October 2019

Acknowledgements

Some of these essays have appeared in other publications.

'Becoming Something Other' in *North & South*, June 2017, pp. 48–54.

'Between Lands', winner of the 2018 Juncture Memoir contest, in *The Walls Between Us: Essays in search of truth* (Philadelphia: Juncture Writing Workshops, 2018), pp. 9–16.

'Ancient Land' in *Headland*, Issue 12, April 2018.

'A Privileged Job' in *Corpus*, 17 October 2016: https://corpus.nz/a-privileged-job/

'A Roof Over Our Heads' in Thom Conroy (ed.), *Home: New writing* (Palmerston North: Massey University Press, 2017), pp. 243–51.

'In the Midst of My True Life', winner of the 2018 Elyne Mitchell Writing Award for non-fiction, in *Elyne Mitchell Writing Awards 2018 Shortlisted Stories* (Victoria: Corryong Neighbourhood Centre, 2018), p. 43–47.

'Love, Loss and the Fraser Basin' in *1964: Mountain culture/Aotearoa*, iss. 3, Winter 2020, pp. 83–87.

'Growing Closer' in *Animal*, 2 September 2019: https://animalliterarymagazine.com/2019/09/02/essay-80/

'The Primitive Hut' in John Walsh (ed.), *10 Stories: Writing about architecture/4* (Auckland: Te Kāhui Whaihanga New Zealand Institute of Architects, 2018), pp. 20–24 (Warren Trust Awards for Architectural Writing).

'Across the Whited Fields' in *North & South*, 15 October 2019, pp. 66–72.

Thanks

A BOOK LIKE THIS arises out of a community of people who are generous with their time and support, and to all of you I offer my grateful thanks.

Thank you to Barry Becker and family for access to Rough Ridge and Mt Ida; to Robert and Rosemary Gardyne and family, and the McKnight family, for access to Blackstone Hill, with special thanks to Robert for his guidance; and to Trevor and Judy Beck for access to Triplet Creek and their knowledge of the district.

To Graeme Male for his company on hikes and for wall-building; to Matt Sole for his passion and knowledge of the land and water of Central Otago; to John Breen for the tour into the wonders and history of the Old Man Range; and the Otago Regional Council scientists for their transport and company the length of the Manuherekia.

For the reflections on the adventure of parenting, thank you to my mother Jeannine Bradley and, as always, to my children Hana, Merrin, Rory, Nick and Evie and all the blessed grandchildren.

Thank you to the writers whose words I have quoted and whose work has inspired me; to Joy Cowley and Grahame Sydney for their nurturing art and generous support; to Jo Wane, whose commission began this book; to Professor Carla Spataro of Rosemont College, and the Highlights Foundation, for the opportunity to teach and learn in America; and to Mike and Rose Riddell for their loving encouragement and the words from Polly.

Thank you to Otago University Press, and to Imogen Coxhead for the gallant journey together editing pages.

Lastly, and firstly, my thanks and love to Brian Turner, a warrior of words, for his company on the bike, in the hills, and along the shining streams.

Jillian Sullivan lives and writes in the Ida Valley, Central Otago. Her 12 published books include creative non-fiction, novels, memoir, short story collections and poetry. She teaches writing workshops in New Zealand and the US. Once the drummer in a women's indie pop band, her passion now is natural building and earth plastering. Her latest book is the memoir *A Way Home*, about building her own strawbale home. (Potton and Burton, 2016).